Sermon Crunch

WRITE A POWERFUL SERMON IN HALF THE TIME

Caleb Breakey

Sermon To Book
SermonToBook.com

Sermon Crunch / Caleb Breakey
ISBN-13: 9780692326916
ISBN-10:069232691X

SermonToBook.com began with a simple belief: that sermons should be touching lives, *not* collecting dust. That's why we turn sermons into high-quality books that are accessible to people all over the globe.

Turning your sermon or sermon series into a book exposes more people to God's Word, better equips you for counseling, accelerates future sermon prep, adds credibility to your ministry, and even helps make ends meet during tight times.

John 21:25 tells us that the world itself couldn't contain the books that would be written about the work of Jesus Christ. Our mission is to try anyway. Because, in Heaven, there will no longer be a need for sermons or books. Our time is now.

If God so leads you, we'd love to work with you on your sermon or sermon series.

Visit SermonToBook.com to learn more.

Take our survey at <u>SermonToBook.com</u> to see if your sermons are ready for a book!

- **Impact** your church, community, and the entire world with sermons you've already preached.

- **Discover** how to publish your sermons in less than 1 hour of your time.

- **Learn** the process we use to help pastors fund their books before they are even written.

Contents

Once again Caleb Breakey is using his gifts to serve the church. *Sermon Crunch* is a simple yet profound tool that will help every preacher improve his sermon preparation and delivery. Get this little book and implement the 7 Structural Pillars to preach God's Word with power.

—Steve Marfia, Lead Pastor, Legacy 242, New Jersey; Founder and President, NewGround Ministries

Caleb Breakey's *Sermon Crunch* is a must-have resource for the student and the seasoned preacher. This book is full of practical principles that will lead you through the process of effective sermon preparation that engages and compels an audience to action. I definitely plan on having my preachers get this book as part of their ministerial training.

—Steve Bozeman, Lead Pastor, New Beginnings Church of Atlanta

Sermon Crunch has three key qualities I value in a book: clarity, brevity, and usefulness. It's a resource that will greatly benefit every new pastor, and many old pastors as well!

—Josh Kelley, Speaker and Author of Radically Normal

With many a speaker being less than clear on his points and structure, *Sermon Crunch* will be very helpful. In terms of homiletics, it will help the teacher and listener engage, track, and be interested.

—Mark Lind, Associate Pastor, Spring Creek Bible Church

This Book Doesn't Write Your Sermon for You

"If there is no power it is not preaching. True preaching, after all, is God acting. It is not just a man uttering words; it is God using him. He is being used of God. He is under the influence of the Holy Spirit." — **Martyn Lloyd-Jones**

BEFORE WE GET INTO the meat of *Sermon Crunch*, let's spit out the gristle.

The idea of cutting your sermon prep in half has nothing to do with slapping together a half-hearted sermon so you can play Solitaire in your office all week. The goal of *Sermon Crunch* isn't to give God less time and expect the same result. Nor is it to add rules to the neglect of the Spirit, cut back on preparation or prayer, emphasize efficiency over labor and effort, or try to manufacture a spiritual "meal."

I want to be clear. *Sermon Crunch* doesn't save you time *receiving* your message, (i.e. reading the text, praying, meditating, doing word studies, cross-referencing, reading commentaries, studying culture and historical background), but it certainly saves you time *arranging* your message.

Excellent preaching thrives where Spirit dependence meets laborious and intentional preparation, which is why I'm an advocate of pastors taking as long as they need to transfer what God has placed on their hearts into the hearts of their congregation.

I like how pastor and author Josh Kelley puts it: "It's my job to offer the Holy Spirit the best possible tools I can, which He then uses to work on the hearts of the listener."

This book is about those "best possible tools."

Why Do I Need *Sermon Crunch?*

Do you know what to preach, but struggle organizing your sermon in the most powerful way possible? Do you sometimes feel like your congregation is bored with your preaching style? Do you wish there were more impactful ways to present illustrations? Do you wonder if your sermons lack practical elements that can be applied in daily life? Do you get frustrated trying to connect your message with the needs of your flock? If you resonated with any of these questions, *Sermon Crunch* will be an invaluable tool for you.

In the following chapters, I will teach you 7 award-winning structural pillars to strengthen your sermon prep, organization and delivery. These pillars reduce the stress and time it takes to assemble your message, not to mention spark creative ways to enhance your preaching style.

The organizational pillars in this book were fashioned from ten years of studying powerful communication. They have achieved prestigious awards and operate as the blueprint for several authors and public speakers. But the beauty of *Sermon Crunch* is that it takes these pillars and tailors them uniquely for pastors.

And don't worry. They go deeper than the basic introduction/body/conclusion that you learned in fifth grade.

> *"Lack of and carelessness in the matter of arrangement is one of the most common faults of preaching today. It ought to be considered inexcusable, because it implies a lack of labor and an unwillingness to spend time on the sermon. Laziness is a sin many preachers need to repent of and forsake."* — **William Evans, How to Prepare Sermons**

Let's Be Real

If you're like most pastors, time is like gold: precious, rare, and hard to come by. Let me ask you a question. In a given week, how often do you think:

- *Am I going to be able to finish my sermon on time?*

- *Oh no, another drop in. I'll never be ready for Sunday.*

- *How am I going to juggle my family commitments on Saturday, when I'm not finished preparing my message for Sunday?*

- *I've studied and prayed and I finally have my material compiled...but how in the world should I organize it?*

The goal of *Sermon Crunch* is to help you overcome these anxious thoughts by streamlining the sermon prep process. Instead of struggling over what bullet points go where, *Sermon Crunch* makes organizing your information as simple as drag-and-drop.

"A sermon needs an outline just as a man needs a skeleton." — **William Evans, How to Prepare Sermons**

The 7 Structural Pillars and What's To Come

Snatch Our Attention
Simplify The Point
Help Us See Why
Give Us Proof
Articulate Our Questions
Show Us How
Inspire Us To Go

Each of these pillars is intimately connected to a singular purpose: to help your congregation receive God's Word in the most impacting and life-changing way possible.

The first seven chapters of *Sermon Crunch* offer vital information on why it is important to incorporate these techniques into your weekly (and yearly) sermon preparation. Each chapter poses questions and suggests action items that, if used, will streamline your planning and encourage you to think critically about the different areas of your message.

For example, I may ask you to consider the spiritual condition of your congregation before writing your conclusion, or your church's culture before including a particular sermon illustration.

After working through the 7 pillars (Chapters 1-7), Chapter 8 presents some invaluable tools to "take back your week." I've included ideas for how to schedule each week in order to allow for plenty of relaxed sermon preparation time—without letting necessary church activities fall to the wayside. This chapter also includes a section on creating a yearly *Sermon Calendar*. Investing just a small amount time to create this calendar will eliminate wasted time in the long run—positively impacting both your family and your congregation.

Then, in Chapter 9 I address a tender topic: sermon criticism. You will be encouraged and equipped for *how* to deal with criticism...because criticism will come! I also address some of the reasons why people from your congregation complain, and move you toward responding with the heart of God when sharp arrows come your way.

Chapter 10 will equip you for refining your sermon before actually preaching it on Sunday—*in one cup of coffee.* This chapter includes practical information on revising your message using the 7 structural pillars I have suggested, with the help of a trusted friend.

Finally, in Chapter 11, we'll revisit the utmost importance of prayer in the preacher's life.

Will Sermon Crunch Work for You?

Only you can know if *Sermon Crunch* will help you. But I'm confident that the value gleaned from this organizational tool far outweighs the investment of time required to read it.

God tells us that there is blessing for ordering our days. Paul writes, "…all things should be done decently and in order" (1 Corinthians 14:40, ESV).

Throughout history, God has spoken to His people through appointed leaders. He raised up Moses to declare His Word to His people. He ordained prophets to remind His people of His law and covenants, and to call His people to return to Him. These appointed mouthpieces stood firm in their calling to receive the Word and preach it. No doubt, their lives were impacted by what God was calling them to do. They experienced persecution, burnout and criticism. You will too. This book will give you tools to help prevent and deal with these issues.

People sitting in the pews today desperately need to hear the word of Christ. It is a matter of life or death.

"So then faith cometh by hearing, and hearing by the word of God." — **Romans 10:17**

You, pastor, are a guardian of the gospel (2 Timothy 1:14; 2:2) for three reasons: to hold firmly to the faithful Word, to refute those who might contradict it or distort it, and to pass it along to the next generation (Titus 1:5–9). You are but one of a long lineage of mouthpieces for God entrusted to guard the deposit. You are commissioned to pass the baton to younger leaders who will do the same. Your message has the possibility of impacting generations. In short, your preaching *matters*.

It is a fulfilling and overwhelming job. It is both rewarding and draining. It takes hard work, perseverance and a large dose of faith. And it takes the commitment of fellow leaders who will come alongside and help you with a job that is far too big for one person. Time is short and people are desperate for purpose and meaning in life. And God has chosen you for such a time as this.

There is no time for laziness or a lack of motivation, and there is certainly no time for disorganization. There is work to be done, and God's Word says there is an orderly way to progress forward.

Our hope is that the tools in this book will help reduce the hours you are putting into sermon preparation, so that you might be able to better fulfill the calling God has placed on your life. I pray this resource will help you be able to continue running the race set out for you with joy and anticipation for what is ahead.

Seek God in everything, especially when preparing your sermon. There are souls at stake, and the job is big. *Sermon Crunch* offers a structured, disciplined way to approach each day and week, so that you don't burn out in the process.

> *"Do you not know that in a race all the runners run, but only one gets the prize? Run in such a way as to get the prize. Everyone who competes in the games goes into strict training. They do it to get a crown that will not last, but we do it to get a crown that will last forever." — 1 Corinthians 9:24-27*

Are you ready to implement the 7 structural pillars outlined in *Sermon Crunch* and transform how you prepare and deliver your sermons? Then let's dive in.

> *"The musician studies the rules of expression and harmony; the painter studies the mechanism of his art ... So, too, does the preacher need to study the art of sermon construction, the psychology of an audience and the principles of delivery." — **T.H. Scambler, The Art of Sermon Construction***

Will Sermon Crunch Work for You?

You'll find several quotes from pastors and authors throughout *Sermon Crunch*, each with a unique opinion regarding how to prepare and deliver a sermon. My goal in including such a broad range of perspectives was not to confuse you, but rather to show that every pastor has personal convictions when it comes to preaching. Thus, as you read each quote, remember Romans 5:14, which says "One person considers one day more sacred than another; another considers every day alike. Each of them should be fully convinced in their own mind."

I hope that *Sermon Crunch*, as a whole, enriches your own unique process and allows for a great deal of Spirit-led latitude as you preach God's Word.

Take our survey at <u>SermonToBook.com</u> to see if your sermons are ready for a book!

1—Snatch Our Attention

*"An audience will not be interested simply because the speaker says, 'Now hear me,' or 'Give me your attention,' or 'Now listen.' It is the business of the public speaker to present his matter so interestingly that the audience cannot help but listen." — **William Evans, How To Prepare Sermons**

JIM AND MARY try to look as composed as possible as they hurry into the church. They hush their talkative toddler, put the binky back in baby's mouth, shake the greeter's hand, and hope they aren't the only family running behind schedule.

Oh, great, Jim thought. *The service has already started, spit up is still on Mary, the only seat available is in the front row, and who knows whether the car will start again after the trouble they had making it to church. Could this week get off to a worse start?*

The worship music started to play…

Unfortunately, Jim and Mary's story is a common one. Whether we mean to or not, many of us in the body of Christ fall into the snare of attending church with our brains half-fried from the stress of the week. The other half is on what to make for lunch, what to do about the broken furnace, why Jim didn't get that promotion, and *who left a wad of gum on the pew?*

Although we are physically present at church, we are mentally weighted down by our trivial—and not so trivial—

burdens. That is why we need you to snatch our attention, pillar number one.

You are equipped with the most captivating material in human history: the very words of God. The question is, are you using them in a way that captivates?

Now, merely getting our attention isn't the point. Any pastor can use an outrageous prop or outlandish story to wow his congregation.

The point is to achieve tasteful attention that builds interest, provokes thought, and gives your congregation a clear reason for why they should slide their worries aside and give you their undivided attention for the next 25-45 minutes. This happens when the attention-grabber points to Jesus.

More practically, it happens when scriptural truth meets our pain, reveals our sin, or reflects our deep need for Christ.

As you're preparing your sermon, ask yourself:

When prepping, ask:

- How does the text meet my congregation's pain?

- Where does the text reveal the sin my congregation is fighting against?

- How does the text reflect my congregation's deep need for Jesus?

Prepare your sermon with answers to these questions in mind. This helps frame your message in a way that naturally captivates your congregation from the start.

Let's look at our tired, young parents Jim and Mary again. Imagine you are about to preach on 1 Corinthians 15:58:

> *"Therefore, my dear brothers and sisters, stand firm. Let nothing move you. Always give yourselves fully to the work of the Lord, because you know that your labor in the Lord is not in vain."*

Before framing a sermon outline, ask yourself how this text may:

[handwritten margin note: before framing the sermon, ask]

1. Affirm pain that your congregation might be feeling.
2. Reveal any harbored sin in their hearts.
3. Remind them of their need for Jesus.

Certainly Jim and Mary are laboring as they tend to the everyday troubles of life, such as worrying about money to fix their car, raising young children, and feeling inadequate. Do you think Paul's exhortation to "stand firm" may resonate with their weary souls to press on?

Or perhaps they're struggling with resentment toward one another for not helping enough. Could Paul's words to "let nothing move you" convict their hearts to continue working for the Lord alone, knowing their labor is "not in vain"?

Or could this text be a comforting reminder of their need for Jesus during difficult seasons?

Your goal should be to meet your congregation right where they are the moment you begin preaching. Asking yourself the three questions I shared above will help you reach that goal.

Deciding on a Text

*"The pulpit is the throne of the Word of God. Therefore, the sacred text must be the priority of our preaching." — **H.B. Charles, Jr., On Preaching***

Before you can ask yourself these three important questions, you must have a text in mind to preach on.

It is important to start with a particular scripture, and build your message based on that scripture rather than deciding what you want to communicate and searching to find the perfect verse to support your opinion.

In his book *How to Prepare Sermons*, William Evans lists five reasons preachers should build messages based on scripture:

- Scripture awakens the interest of the audience, and grabs their attention.

- Scripture wins the confidence of the audience. They know what the preacher is saying can be trusted because God's Word backs it up.

- Scripture gives the preacher authority and boldness in the proclamation of the message. There is supernatural power in scriptural texts!

- Scripture keeps the preacher's mind from wandering. It forces him to make all his comments around that particular text.

- Scripture keeps the preacher biblical. It prevents interjecting too much human opinion or cultural prejudices into the sermon.

Understandably, choosing appropriate Scripture from which to preach is paramount. Be careful of teaching odd or confusing texts. Some passages in the Bible are best suited for teaching in an academic environment, and some simply cannot be explained in one sermon. Pray and meditate diligently before preaching any piece of Scripture. Do word studies to see what deeper meaning God may reveal, and examine cross-references.

Also, be aware of taking Scripture out of context. Portions of Scripture can be massacred because the surrounding context has not been examined.

And finally, preach from both the Old and New Testament. There is a richness that comes from looking back to the foundation of everything our New Testament is based on.

Read Diligently

"If you're a serious minded leader, you will read. You will read all you can. You will read when you feel like it, and you will read when you don't." — **Bill Hybels, Axiom: Powerful Leadership Proverbs**

Reading Scripture is of utmost importance for effective sermon preparation. You cannot preach biblically without first reading and digesting the Bible.

Read the text you plan to preach on. Then read it again…and again. Then, read commentaries from various theologians who have studied these passages in depth, including those with whom you hold a different viewpoint. It stretches your thinking, and undergirds your message.

The more you read, the more you glean from the wisdom of others to better understand the text. If you fail to know and understand the text, nothing else in your message matters, regardless of how great your attention grabber may be.

Finally, seek the counsel of trusted friends and spiritual counselors for further wisdom on the meaning of the text.

Nothing Snatches Attention Like This

"Order is of great importance. He who wishes to break a hard rock with his sledge, does not hammer here and there over the surface, but multiplies his blows upon a certain point or along a certain line." — **John A. Broadus, On the Preparation and Delivery of Sermons**

Though there are several ways to begin a sermon—(i.e. declaring a problem, quoting someone you admire, writing a stunning statement, using video or audio, performing an object lesson, describing the background of the text)—nothing grabs attention *while* simultaneously connecting to the soul like story.

Josh Hunt, author of *Teach Like Jesus*, summed up this principle well when he said, "Anytime we do a teaching and don't include a generous helping of stories, we fail to teach like Jesus." Jesus told oodles of stories, and as His representative here on earth 2,000 years later, it is wise to follow what our expert preacher modeled.

[margin note: Jesus told stories]

So as soon as you've identified the pain the text meets, the sin it reveals, or the deep need for Jesus it reflects—or, most likely, a combination of these—think on these questions:

[margin note: After making it ident. of needs, ASK these 3's about the story you want to tell.]

How can I express my message through story? How can this story start with a bang? How can this story go in a direction no one sees coming?

What concrete details can I use to make the story memorable, unique, and genuine?

How can this story open a gap in my congregation's thinking that can be filled with scriptural truth?

Note: Only use story if it naturally fits and complements the text. Otherwise, use one of the other sermon starters mentioned previously.

You may be thinking, where do I find these tales? As I have already encouraged, read voraciously! Have a book nearby at all times, along with a highlighter. Whenever you have down time, read. When you are sitting in the car, waiting to pick up your child at school, read. Have a doctor's appointment? Bring a book for the waiting room. Great stories are found in great books.

David B. Smith, who pastors Upper Room Fellowship in Temple City, California, wrote that he trudged his way through Winston Churchill's 600-page masterpiece, *Their Finest Hour.* Though it was a challenging read, Smith said the book was "overflowing with juicy tales!"

According to Smith:

"Hitler's German High Command had perfected a new 'split beam' kind of radar which was guaranteed to guide the Luftwaffe bombers unerringly to their London targets. Unbeknownst to them, Number Ten Downing Street's scientists had intercepted the technology, and soon managed to throw off just one of the Nazi's beams the tiniest amount. Wave after wave of German bombs landed harmlessly in the wilderness, and the pilots themselves were often knocked off course. The cigar-chomping Prime Minister took evident pleasure and satisfaction in the wartime story of the German bomber who confidently landed in Devonshire, thinking he was in France."

Said Smith of this illustration, "What a picture of how Satan tries to take our earnest spiritual habits and turn them against us!"

Don't just read *Time Magazine* for the news or watch a movie for entertainment. Always be on the lookout for that "hook," that opportunity to connect people to Scripture through a story.

Conduct an online search for sermon illustrations (see Appendix D). There are many online resources that provide stories, anecdotes and quotes that make powerful attention grabbers.

Possibly the best sermon illustrations, however, are found on common ground between the preacher and the audience. Sharing a personal story that your audience has also experienced connects with them on a deep level.

Make a list of personal stories you could use as attention-grabbing sermon starters. As you scan your list, ask yourself hard questions, such as: "Do I just like this story because it makes me look good? Would my congregation be able to relate to this story on a profound level? Does this story really go with my sermon or do I just think it's entertaining?"

Be honest as you evaluate your list and discard stories that don't make the cut.

Then, create some kind of filing system to store your ideas. For your convenience, you can include different tabs like: Baptism, Marriage, Parenting, Christmas, Eschatology, Prayer, Salvation, Sin, and so forth. This will help you immensely when you're down to the wire and need a story to illustrate a certain topic.

Evernote.com offers a wonderful online organization system that syncs across phones and computers. It allows you to clip from anywhere on the web, save inspirational ideas, and share and discuss notes with others.

Pretty soon, you will have a file full of notes and printouts that say, "This story goes with *that* sermon."

According to Smith, lively, edgy, human-interest stories are the glue that holds a great sermon together.

But be careful! Stories can quickly eat up too much time and *lose* your congregation's attention if you can't get out of the starting gate.

Reasons to Tell Stories

Sharing a story is far more powerful than stating some facts. The goal in storytelling is to paint a picture for us through imagery.

Ideas connect to people intellectually, but stories connect to their emotions. According to Brandon Hilgemann, the most powerful sermons connect with people on both an emotional and intellectual level. In addition to this, Hilgemann suggests in his book, *Preaching Nuts & Bolts*, a few other benefits to using stories to illustrate a point in your sermon:

- Stories provide clarity to difficult concepts. Stories put skin on ideas, making them more tangible.

- Stories are memorable long after the sermon is forgotten. How many sermons do you remember from other pastors? How many stories? People naturally recall stories easier than bullet points.

- Stories make hard truths easier to swallow. They can be like sugar coating on a bitter pill. People are more receptive to teaching when they see how it plays out in story.

- Stories capture people's attention. Whether they are funny, exciting, sad or touching, a well-placed story grabs an audience's wandering attention and thrusts it back to the sermon.

- Stories make a pastor human. When you share personal failures, funny moments or hard times from your life, it shows you are human and makes you more relatable. It shows you actually believe what you are preaching and are trying to live it out as best you can.

- Stories allow for easier application. I can tall you to be a good parent, but what exactly does that look like? A story can show exactly what you mean in a very specific life situation.

The Introduction: 20°/.
The Three Important Paragraphs

"Whichever way you begin your message, a strong introduction is essential, necessary and beneficial." — **HB Charles Jr., On Preaching**

The introduction should be about twenty percent of your entire sermon. Though any story you write for the introduction should be longer than a statement or question, it's important to keep it short and to the point. For a solid, attention-grabbing story, I recommend three paragraphs:

- **The Setup:** Orient your congregation to the 5 W's of your story: Who, What, Where, When, and Why.

- **The Incident:** Describe what happens in the story that sets up the point you want to make.

- **The Reveal:** Show how the story connects to the overall point of your message.

Once finished, edit out parts that have no bearing on your sermon. If a story doesn't naturally fit and complement the text, use a different sermon starter.

To see how this formula works, consider the story at the beginning of this chapter about Jim and Mary:

The Setup: Jim and Mary (who) try to look as composed as possible (what) as they hurry into the church (where). They hush their talkative toddler, put the Binky back in baby's mouth, shake the greeter's hand, and hope they aren't the only family running behind schedule.

Oh, great, Jim thought. *The service has already started (when), spit up is still on Mary, the only seat available is in the front row, and who knows whether the car will start again after the trouble they had making it to church. Could this week get off to a worse start (why)?*

The Incident: The worship music started to play...

The Reveal: Unfortunately, Jim and Mary's story is a common one. Whether we mean to or not, many of us in the body of Christ fall into the snare of attending church with our brains half-fried from the stress of the week. The other half is on what to make for lunch, what to do about the broken furnace, why Jim didn't get that promotion, and *who left a wad of gum on the pew?* Although we are physically present at church, we are mentally weighted down by our trivial—and not so trivial—burdens. That is why we need (pastors) to snatch our attention.

The Best Stories Find You

Pastor Joel C. Gregory tells the story of how he visited a student café in central Oxford, UK. At the cash register, a box of clamshells rested with a sign inviting customers to take a clamshell to their tables if they wished to talk with a stranger while eating. Gregory describes how he contemplated this box of clamshells while he ate. The café, he says, sits in the middle of 10,000 of the smartest young adults in the world. Why, he wondered, would such people need to take a clamshell to a café table to bid lunchtime conversation?

He wondered, *should I take a shell? What if I take a shell and nobody comes to talk with me?*

Then he thought, *what if this shell game was a brilliant idea for encouraging connectedness? What if this became a universal custom? What if this simple act to end loneliness was the start of something profound?*

Suddenly, a download of biblical insights poured into Gregory's brain. He thought of the Psalmist's cry in Psalm 25:16: "Turn to me and be gracious to me, because I am lonely and afflicted."

Says Gregory, "Shortly after seeing that clamshell in the café, I knew that this mollusk was going to show up in a sermon."

This is your goal: to look for attention grabbers all the time. Look for them at restaurants or at sporting events. Pay attention for possible illustrations when you are on vacation.

When you are sitting on the couch with your wife and kids, recapping the day, ask yourself: could this be used to illustrate a point? Always be on alert for everyday experiences that grab the heart of your congregation and help them relate to the message you are communicating. You don't find the very best stories; the very best stories find you (*The Preachers Complete Skills Guide,* Christianity Today International).

There are many other ways to start a sermon, beyond telling a story. According to Cornelius Platinga in his book *Reading for Preaching*, the term is actually a catch-all for anecdotes, analogies, stories, blog entries, editorial opinions, famous tweets, incidents from history, memorable sayings, biographical profiles, statistics, snippets of dialogue from TV interviews, lines from Wikipedia bios, lines from poems, news reports, people's comments on news reports, summaries of film plots, or sentences from one of Bonheoffer's prison letters. It involves all of the other fine things preachers gather, store, and retrieve in order to dress their interpreted text properly so that when Sunday morning comes the preacher's sermon may appear "clothed and in [its] right mind" (Cornelius Platinga, *Reading for Preaching*).

The importance of snatching your congregation's attention applies no matter what illustration method you chose. And though you may hit a home run with your attention grabber, always remember in your possession is the most captivating material on the planet. Never let an illustration take the place of the Word of God.

*"Whichever way you begin your message, a strong introduction is essential, necessary, and beneficial." — **H.B. Charles Jr., On Preaching***

Chapter Summary:

It is paramount that you consider the emotions of your congregation—their pain, their sin and the need for Christ—when choosing the text you preach on. *How* you handle this text in the first few minutes of your sermon will make or break whether you have the attention of your audience for the remainder of your message. Always use Scripture as your main attention grabber, your "hook," but make good use of stories that connect to the Scripture you are teaching on. Look for stories and illustrations online, in media, in books and in magazines, and organize them for easy retrieval in the future.

Next, you'll need to work on *Simplifying Your Point*, the second structural pillar.

Take our survey at SermonToBook.com to see if your sermons are ready for a book!

Snatch Our Attention

Write an attention-grabbing story in three paragraphs: The Setup, The Incident, and The Reveal. Once finished, edit out parts that have no bearing on your sermon. If a story doesn't naturally fit and complement the text, use a different sermon starter.

2—Simplify the Point

"The preacher should have only one theme in his sermon and concentrate all his argument, proof, testimony, illustration, and so on, toward the enforcing of that theme." —
William Evans, How to Prepare Sermons

THE COACH TAPPED THE BOY'S ELBOW in between pitches during batting practice.

"Move this up a little more," he said. "Good. Now I want you to keep your back leg planted and pivot when you hit the ball. That's where you get your power."

The coach started back toward the coaching box, and then added, "One more thing. Keep your head steady. It's flailing a little bit. So keep it steady and watch the ball all the way to the bat."

Fifty-six words, five commands. That's how coaches speak during practice.

But during a game? They simply nod their heads, clap twice, and say five words: "Hit the ball hard somewhere." They simplify the objective into an easy-to-understand statement that the player can repeat in his head between every pitch.

This is how sermons need to be.

If we leave church without an easy-to-understand statement that sums up your sermon's objective—then we're stepping to the plate in a mental fog instead of just hitting the ball.

"We must strive not merely to render it possible that the people should understand us, but impossible that they should misunderstand." — **John A. Broadus, On the Preparation and Delivery of Sermons**

So as soon as you've snatched our attention with an engaging story, you must simplify the point of the sermon.

It's not that we're not sophisticated enough to handle five points that start with P. It's that we live in Constant Information Overload. Our brains are scientifically rewiring as we speak because the world in which we operate has changed. So ask yourself:

How can I sum up my sermon in a sentence?

Squeezing an entire sermon into one sentence may sound impossible. But if you can't write out what you intend to say in one sentence, you most likely don't have a definite idea of what you are going to be preaching.

This one-line sermon is sometimes referred to as the "the big idea." In this book, I call it the *Sermon Summary Sentence.* A strong, well-designed Sermon Summary Sentence embodies the crux of what your message is about. The rest of your material—the expanded content, the application, and depth of meaning—comes later.

Ask yourself the following questions about the passage you are going to preach on to help you arrive at your Sermon Summary Sentence:

- *How* would you explain the passage you are going to preach to a middle-school child?

- *What* three words immediately come to mind when you think of this passage?

- *What* phrase jumps out at you in the text?

- *Why* is this passage important for your listeners to understand?

After answering these questions, write them down. Many times a few words within a text can culminate in to an entire sermon! Spend some time asking the Holy Spirit for direction. As you study your text, God will reveal your Sermon Summary Sentence and the message He wants to give both you and your entire congregation.

The following are some strong Sermon Summary Sentences, based off a particular piece of Scripture:

James 1: Trials occur, but God promises blessing to those who remain steadfast.

Joshua 1:3-9: Those who trust God and obey His Word have nothing to fear in this world.

Sometimes coming up with the Sermon Summary Sentence is the hardest part of writing your sermon. How do you know when you have it?

When you can summarize your entire sermon in one sentence!

"Expository preaching is the communication of a biblical concept. A sermon should be a bullet, not buckshot. Ideally, each sermon is the explanation, interpretation or application of a single dominant idea supported by other ideas, all drawn from one passage, or several passages of Scripture."
— **Haddon Robinson, Biblical Preaching**

Taking It A Step Further

Certain phrases stick with us. Maybe not word for word, but the idea cuts through the frontal lobe of the brain and cements itself in there for good. For instance, note these Scriptures in italics:

- **Proverbs 16:8:** "*Pride goes before destruction*, a haughty spirit before a fall."

- **Proverbs 27:17:** "As *iron sharpens iron*, so one person sharpens another."

- **Proverbs 31:30:** *"Charm is deceptive, and beauty is fleeting;* but a woman who fears the LORD is to be praised."

This is the kind of Sermon Summary Sentence you should strive for. Not just a simple sentence, but a vivid description or poetic adage that sticks.

Consider the difference between the following one-sentence sermon summaries:

A changed heart gives a new start

When your heart changes, your life becomes new.

Which of the two will stick? Though both describe the heart transformation that happens to the believer in Christ, the first Sermon Summary Sentence, "A changed heart gives a new start" is proverbial-like and memorable.

 Ask yourself the following three questions when creating a one-sentence sermon summary:

- *Is my sermon summary easy to remember?*

- *How can I turn my sermon summary into a proverb-like saying that is catchy?*

- *Does it capture the message God wants my congregation to receive?*

Simplifying your point when summing up your sermon's objective sends your listeners home with a clear message they will remember well past Sunday.

> *"A word fitly spoken is like apples of gold in settings of silver"* — **Proverbs 25: 11**

Chapter Summary:

After snatching your audience's attention, you must simplify your point by creating a one-sentence summary of your sermon, or a Sermon Summary Sentence. This sentence should be written like a catchy proverb. It should be easy to remember, simple and it should *stick* with us!

Once you have your Sermon Summary Sentence solidified, it is important to consider *why* your message is so important for us. We'll examine that next in Chapter 4 when we address why it is important for you to *Help Us See Why*, the third pillar.

Take our survey at SermonToBook.com to see if your sermons are ready for a book!

Simplify The Point

Write a sermon summary sentence. Then, turn it into a Proverb-like saying. Consider using comparison, contrast, or rhyme. Ideally, it should connect flawlessly with the Reveal of your attention-grabbing story. Consider repeating this Proverb-like saying several times throughout your sermon. (Also great for brainstorming your sermon title).

TIP

3—Help Us See Why

*"Preaching ought to be not merely convincing and persuasive, but eminently instructive." — **John A. Broadus, On the Preparation and Delivery of Sermons***

PASTORS EVERYWHERE should familiarize themselves with the concept in Simon Sinek's book, *Start With Why*. If Simon were to speak at a pastor's conference, he might share the following insight about the pulpit:

Pastors everywhere know *what* they do. They preach the Word of God every Sunday in a place of worship and shepherd their flocks.

These pastors also know *how* they do what they do (i.e. morning service, evening service, weekly classes, counseling, and hospital and home visits).

But few pastors can clearly articulate *why* they preach what they preach on any given week. Sure they can say, "It's about Jesus." But when it comes to the specifics of why their sermons are important and beneficial to their flock, they offer little. And this can have a devastating effect on the congregation.

This is why once you've snatched our attention and simplified the point, you must help us see *why* your sermon is so vital and beneficial to us as humans and followers of Christ.

The Two Critical Paragraphs

"I take my text and make a beeline to the cross." — **Charles H. Spurgeon**

A pastor recently embraced the idea of *helping people see why* before addressing a group of high school students about sexual purity.

They'd been told to wait until marriage multiple times. They'd been encouraged to sign contracts and wear purity rings. But they'd never been clearly shown why God commands that the marriage bed be holy.

So the pastor set out to work on the *why*.

First, he looked over his simplified point of his sermon: "Purity isn't just about *not doing sinful things*, but *waiting for the best thing.*" (Don't miss that catchy Sermon Summary Sentence!) Then he wrote down the top three biblical ways that "waiting for the best thing" benefited their lives:

- **First Blessing:** Remaining pure is a way to actively worship God (*Romans 12:1*).

- **Second Blessing:** Staying physically unblemished is obedience to God, which inspires numerous physical and emotional benefits (*Hebrews 13:4).*

- **Third Blessing:** A pure heart flows into every other part of our lives (*Proverbs 4:23*).

Next, the pastor wrote a *Blessings Paragraph* based on the top three benefits to help young people understand the importance of purity:

- *The Blessings Paragraph:* By the end of this sermon, you'll discover how to worship God with your body, stay physically unblemished, and be committed to purity and the inner heart of a person, rather than being a prisoner to lust and outer appearance.

After that, he revealed the consequences that occur when you don't follow God's commands for purity.

1) **First Consequence:** When you sin against your body, your worship of God becomes muddled and your ability to point others to Jesus deteriorates (*1 Corinthians 6:18*).

2) **Second Consequence:** On top of feeling an ache in your bones and the heavy conviction of the Holy Spirit (*Psalm 32:3*), you need to discuss your sexual sin with your future other and live with the consequences.

3) **Third Consequence:** A heart corrupted with impurity flows into every other part of your life, and makes you

more susceptible to lusting after the outer appearance than to purity and the inner heart.

Using these three consequence points, the pastor then wrote the *Consequences Paragraph*:

- *The Consequences Paragraph:* When you're sinning against your body, worshiping God and helping others follow Jesus crawls to a halt. You feel an ache in your bones and the heavy conviction of the Holy Spirit. On top of this, you realize that some day you have to discuss your sexual sin with your future other and live with the consequences. And finally, you feel the excruciating flow of your corrupted heart pour into every other part of your life, making you more susceptible to lusting after the outer appearance.

When you are equipped with a *Blessings Paragraph* and *Consequences Paragraph*, you are in an excellent position to help us see the *why* of your sermon.

Once you have solidified your *Sermon Summary Sentence*, begin writing your *Blessings Paragraph* and *Consequences Paragraph*. This helps your congregation see why your sermon is very important and beneficial to their lives.

To write a Blessing Paragraph:

- Write down the top two or three blessings seen within this Scripture, or that result from a certain action or behavior

From this list, construct a short paragraph on the *blessings* that come from what you are teaching on in the text.

Next, to write a Consequences Paragraph:

- Write down two or three consequences that are within this Scripture, or that results from a certain action or behavior

From this list, construct a short paragraph on the *consequences* that may result.

After this exercise, you should be able to clearly communicate *why* your sermon is very important and beneficial for people sitting under your teaching.

"It is a pity when a sermon lacks coherence or plan. Good ideas may be lost by the hearer, interesting illustrations may fail to admit the light, and choice language may seem pointless, all because the sermon followed no principle of construction." — **T.H. Scambler, The Art of Sermon Construction**

Chapter Summary:

It is imperative that we understand *why* your message is so valuable to our life. Writing out Blessings and Consequences Paragraphs simplifies possible blessings and consequences revealed in a particular passage. It invites us to engage with the particular Scripture you are teaching on, for a *reason*.

Next, we will reflect on the fourth pillar: Why everything coming from your mouth must be grounded in God's Word and affirmed by other godly men and women who've gone before you. Chapter 4 challenges you to *Give Us Proof.*

Take our survey at SermonToBook.com to see if your sermons are ready for a book!

Help Us See Why

Write a Blessings Paragraph and Consequences Paragraph that help your congregation see why your sermon is very important and beneficial to their lives.

4—Give Us Proof

"Ultimately, there are only two ways to preach—by exposition or by imposition. Either your preaching explains the God-intended meaning of the text or it sinfully imposes human speculation onto the text." — **H.B. Charles Jr., On Preaching**

IF A LETTER ARRIVES at your doorstep with the Presidential Seal stamped on it, you would take it more seriously than coupons from Costco.

If a star athlete eats a certain food or drinks a particular beverage, you are more inclined to follow suit.

If millions of people watch a clip online, you're more likely to do the same.

People want proof before they purchase. This is human nature. And it's your job to show us that everything coming from your mouth is grounded in God's Word and affirmed by other godly men and women who've gone before you.

In Acts 17:10-11, the Bereans eagerly received the Word of God from Paul but they also examined the Scriptures daily to see if his words lined up with Scripture. Unfortunately, many believers today put more trust in the pastor than they do in studying God's Word. This is why you must constantly show us that what you're saying from the pulpit aligns with the Bible.

If you don't, you run the risk of us following *you* instead of Jesus. And that's a position no one should envy upon Christ's return.

2 Timothy 2:15 says, "Do your best to present yourself to God as one approved, a worker who has no need to be ashamed, rightly handling the word of truth."

This is why you must give us *proof.*

Proof comes in the form of Scripture, quotes from students of Scripture (i.e. pastors, authors, and historians), statistics and research.

However, don't let the thought of providing proof bog you down. You don't have to spend fifteen minutes explaining everyone's stance on the text or topic at hand. All you need to do is show us that you're using the Word of God as your guide.

Begin with looking for supporting Scripture from the Bible. Ask yourself:

- *Which verses serve as the backbone of my message?*

- *Have I taken any verses out of context?*

- *Do any of these verses require further explanation before I use them as proof?*

List these verses out, and spend time studying and meditating on them. Decide whether they truly support your Sermon Summary Sentence, or if they could become unnecessary filler verses. Including Scripture for the sake of including Scripture misses something profoundly important.

Steven Lawson writes that each time a preacher opens the Scripture, he must be acutely aware that he is opening the Word of the living God. Writes Lawson, "He must never allow himself to come to the Bible callously or out of empty routine. Rather, his heart should always be gripped with the profound truth that God is speaking in the text."

If God affirms the verses you have chosen as appropriate for communicating His message to your congregation, incorporate them.

Remember: the podium is not your soapbox. Preach the Word accurately and communicate the truths of God as given in His Word.

Proof, Proof, And More Proof

"Our preaching is not the reason the Word works. The Word is the reason our preaching works." — **H.B. Charles Jr., On Preaching**

Next, dive into your favorite authors and commentaries to discover what they have to say about your sermon topic.

Ask yourself:

- *Which books and articles can I draw from?*

- *Do the quotes I want to use fit the context of my message?*

- *Do any of them need further clarification before using them in my sermon?*

Then, begin to add these to the skeleton of your message. Guard against dumping a scattered collection of grammatical findings and quotations from various sources into your outline that do not connect to your overall message. Remember your Sermon Summary Sentence? Make sure everything you add supports this sentence.

Combine these elements, along with the supporting Scripture you have chosen, into a smooth, fluid, interesting and gripping message.

Finally, consider what research and statistics say about your topic. Ask yourself:

- *Is there relevant research I've yet to include?*

- *Are my sources credible?*

- *Are the statistics reliable and up-to-date?*

- *Do I need to qualify anything before I present it?*

A word of caution: it is important that commentary never replaces the Word of God. Your message must always find its sole source in Scripture through careful exegesis, and interpreting it in its ordinary sense and context. You must clearly explain God's intended meaning of the verse—not yours or another commentator's—while also giving Scriptural meaning and application for today.

Where to Find this "Proof"

Outside of hard copy books and commentaries, there are numerous online software programs you can consult. These resources offer help with Greek and Hebrew word studies, charts and outlines, biblical encyclopedias and dictionaries, timelines, devotionals and articles. The following are theologically-sound online resources:

BlueLetterBible.com

Blue Letter Bible is an online interactive reference library continuously updated from the teachings and commentaries of selected pastors and teachers. It includes commentaries, concordances, dictionaries, encyclopedias, articles, videos and lexicons.

BibleStudyTools.com

This website provides an interlinear Bible that syncs with BST Greek and Hebrew fonts; it also offers helpful study tools for free—including commentaries, concordances, dictionaries, encyclopedias, and lexicons.

BibleGateway.com

This easy-to-use Bible searching website allows you to search for passages of Scripture in multiple versions quickly (and painlessly!)

Books.google.com

Google Books allows you to search an entire book, making it an extremely useful database.

Scholar.google.com

What Google Books does for books, Google Scholar does for journals. This site turns up helpful information, especially if you're looking for journal articles on a given topic.

ccel.org

Christian Classics Ethereal Library is the largest collection of historic Christian resources on the Internet. If you need information on church fathers such as Augustine, Aquinas, Calvin, or the Puritans, CCEL is a great first place to look.

In addition, there are about two-dozen classic commentary sets available online. One of the most expansive lists, organized by book of the Bible, can be found at *www.DeeperStudy.com.*

Including commentary, history, biographies or quotations helps give proof to your message. However, always prioritize the truth of Scripture, and deemphasize others' opinions. Only God's Word can change the hearts of the people in your congregation.

*"It is clear that you cannot preach the Word if you do not actually use the Word in your preaching." — **H.B. Charles Jr., On Preaching***

Chapter Summary:

I have encouraged you to support your message with proof, such as Scripture, quotes from other students of Scripture (i.e. pastors, authors, and historians), statistics and research. I've also encouraged you to make sure God's Word is prioritized over any commentary or research you may share with us in your sermon. This proof makes you a credible preacher to us, and engages us even more in your message.

Articulating our questions before we ask them—the fifth pillar—communicates your interest in our lives. This is the next step in writing your sermon, and the focus of Chapter 5. Let's continue!

Take our survey at SermonToBook.com to see if your sermons are ready for a book!

Give Us Proof

Write down at least three core verses, three quotes, and one statistic/research nugget that serve as the backbone of your message. Then write a paragraph that sums up your burden of proof. Most likely, there will be overlap with the Help Us See Why section. Keep in mind that the three verses / three quotes / one research statistic is just a suggestion. There is no end to the amount of research that can go into a sermon.

5—Articulate Our Questions

"Express (questions/objections) precisely as you believe it to be in the hearer's mind, so that, listening to your exposition of it, he may say to himself, 'That is exactly my objection; that is precisely my difficulty, and I should wish very much to hear how the preacher will clear it up.'" — **John A. Broadus, On the Preparation and Delivery of Sermons**

QUESTIONS ARE LIKE WEEDS. They begin small and harmless, but soon overtake the entire lawn.

After a while, they're all you see.

When we start formulating questions in the middle of your sermon, we stop listening to the heart of your message because we become distracted by the weeds. The only way to prevent the weeds from sprouting is to cut them off at the root.

How? By articulating our questions before we even know they exist.

For example, imagine that authors Greg D. Gilbert and Sebastian Traeger were preaching a message based on their book, _The Gospel At Work_. Before getting into all the reasons why the congregation should work as working unto the Lord in everything they do, Gilbert and Traeger might start by articulating the questions most of the congregation hasn't thought to ask yet, such as:

"What's the point of work, anyway, in a Christian's life? Is there any meaning to it beyond providing goods and services, making money, and providing a living for my family and myself? And why, for that matter, does God have us spend so much of our lives doing this one particular thing?"

These are questions the congregation is already asking—consciously or subconsciously—in their daily lives. Articulating them before the flock does is similar to a waiter refilling your water before you even realized it was low. It lets us know that you've identified our needs and struggles, and it gives us the assurance that you've searched God's Word for *His* solution.

Empathy is at the core of articulating our questions: it's the act of stepping into our shoes to feel what we're feeling and to address our momentary needs. This isn't just a structural aspect of your sermon. It's a principal rooted in the way of Jesus, who said exactly what people needed to hear the moment they needed to hear it.

We cannot fully engage with you until we know you're fully interested in our concerns. This connection happens when you articulate our questions before we have the opportunity to do it ourselves.

Not All Questions Are Created Equal

There are four kinds of questions you should consider before preaching your sermon:

- Questions your congregation doesn't realize they're already asking (example above).

- Questions that arise from different doctrinal/theological positions.

- Questions that arise from deep hurt.

- Questions that arise from words or concepts people don't understand.

I've already given an example of the first kind of question. Now let's address the second.

Questions that arise from different doctrinal/theological positions: One of our deep needs as humans is to be heard and understood. This is why it's so important for you to think through the doctrinal and theological differences we may hold concerning the text/subject of your sermon.

Even though people join your congregation and claim to align with your understanding and interpretation of Scripture, variations and nuances always exist. No church on the planet can claim that the entire congregation dots every *i* and crosses every *t* in doctrinal and theological matters. And in some cases, there's a wide range of beliefs in the gray areas of Scripture.

The point of addressing doctrinal/theological differences isn't to water down biblical truth with relativism. It's to **1)** recognize that other viewpoints exist—even in your congregation; **2)** restate why you land where *you* do doctrinally/theologically on the text/subject at hand; and **3)** encourage us to always search the Scriptures like a good Berean (Acts 17:11).

By addressing the questions that arise from different doctrinal/theological positions, recasting your own doctrine/theology and prompting us to be full-fledged students of the Bible, you tastefully accomplish several things:

- You make those who interpret the passage differently feel understood.

- You stand firm in the way the Holy Spirit has led you.

- You motivate us to investigate what God's revealed Word says without pushing us away because of differences.

Keep this in mind, though. I'm talking about gray areas of Scripture, *not* core pillars of the Christian faith that are non-negotiable as followers of Jesus, such as the preeminence of Christ, or salvation by grace through faith alone. It would be tragic to make us feel understood in our blindness without imploring us to run to the light.

Questions that arise from deep hurt: There will be days when the subject of your sermon strikes a deep cord with one or more people in your congregation even before you say a word.

Someone may see the title of your sermon—*Your Problems Have Purpose,* for instance (credit: Pastor Steve Bozeman)—

and feel an almost overwhelming pain because he or she just found out their spouse has been unfaithful for the past six months.

This doesn't mean you should change the subject of your sermon or tread lightly on the truth of the Bible. It means you should lean into your sermon all the more with the supernatural compassion of the Holy Spirit, seeking His guidance for how to communicate a difficult subject.

Ask yourself:

- *Who's going to really feel this sermon?*

- *Who might wince at the subject matter because it's just so raw?*

- *How can I take a moment to make them feel totally understood and empower them with the truth that they are not alone?*

Acknowledging people's pain helps alleviate any perceived disconnect between you and the people in your congregation. Though there may be hundreds of people sitting in the pews, people will feel like you are speaking directly to them.

Questions that arise from words or concepts people don't understand: Without realizing it, you may be using fancy theological words to describe something in your sermon, like "Sanctification," "Transubstantiation," "Incarnation," or any other term you learned in seminary. Dubbed *Christianese* by some people, these are words that seasoned Christians use in everyday conversation, but bewilder those who are not-yet-believers or new to the faith. Even words like "gospel" or "glory" may be foreign to some people.

Pastor Brandon Hilgemann lightheartedly jokes that "if there is an '*–ation*' in the word, you better define it or pick a different word."

We should not need a biblical dictionary or encyclopedia to figure out what you are trying to teach us. If you use a big word that we don't understand, you may move on while we are still scratching our heads, asking, "What does that word 'regeneration' mean, anyhow?" *And you've lost us.*

Anticipate this when you are prepping. Ask yourself:

- Am I using any words that might not be clear to someone new to the faith?

- Am I using any words or phrases that might not be clear to a middle school student?

- Am I using any words that end in '*–ation*'?

There is nothing wrong with using technical terms, but explain what you mean every time or you may hear more than one snore from the audience. Don't assume everyone sitting in your pews is on the same page. Most of them probably aren't.

As you write your message, step into the shoes of the most diverse group of five members in your congregation. What questions might they ask during your sermon? Articulate these and make it your aim to find God's answer by your sermon's end.

Next, think of possible painful situations your listeners may be experiencing that may intimately connect to your message. Write two or three affirming sentences acknowledging the possibility of this pain, and a sentence or two of comfort. Incorporate these sentences into your sermon. It makes the person in pain feel understood, and "seen."

Look for points in your sermon where doctrinal or theological differences may come into play. How can you make members of your congregation feel understood and cared for, without disregarding their conflicting viewpoint? Work these into your sermon, too.

And finally, clarify any words or phrases that may be unclear or need defining.

Taking the time to consider these four types of questions that may arise alleviates any question marks in your listeners' minds, before they creep in.

What To Do With Other Questions

Finally, there are questions that don't fit into any of these three categories of questions. What are you to do with those?

I like how John A. Broadus puts it: "We must not waste time in the refutation of trifling objections," he says, "nor mention objections which would never trouble the minds of the hearers, and which furnish no sufficient ground for doubting the truth."

In other words, you should consider the three kinds of questions explored in this chapter with great care. But when it comes to other questions, your best bet is to leave them alone (unless particularly prompted by the Holy Spirit).

Anticipate Questions by Considering Learning Styles

Pastor Joe has prepared a powerful message on sin. He has spent many hours in prayer, and prepared a sound message using the 7 pillars in this book. His introduction is strong—his attention grabber (in his humble opinion) was one of his best yet. He has simplified his point, considered how to help his congregation see *why*, and given plenty of supporting proof.

He scans the pews and sees many people scribbling out notes and nodding with him in agreement as he confidently expounds his message. However, some are staring out the window, glazed over, and a handful of people are clearly taking the opportunity to catch up on lost sleep. Why such a difference in people's engagement?

Consider how *you* learn best. Are you a visual learner? Do you learn best through pictures, diagrams or images? Or are you more logical and mathematical, using reasoning, systems or sequences to retain information? Now consider your audience. Even a small congregation includes individuals who each learn differently. Take a look at the variety of different learning styles below:

Visual/Spatial: These people think in terms of pictures. They use diagrams and colors to help them learn, often replacing words with pictures in their minds. They use color to highlight major or minor conncetion points.

Musical/Auditory: These people prefer sound, music or even rhythms to help them learn. They use mnemonics such as acrostics or jingles to retain information, or put a difficult concept to the tune of a song.

Physical/Kinesthetic: These people use their hands, body and sense of touch to help them learn. They use physical objects to retain information, or write or draw diagrams.

Solitary: These people learn best by studying alone. Their thoughts have a large influence on their performance.

Social: These people learn best in community. Explaining things to or studying with a group helps them learn.

Logical/Mathematical: People who are logical and mathematical use logic, systems and sequences to help them learn. These folks create lists with key points from the material, and seek to understand the *reasons* behind the content presented.

Verbal: Verbal learners prefer to use words both in speech and writing to retain information. Reading content aloud solidifies information in their brains. Role-play is key for these folks.

Learning styles change the way a person internally represents certain experiences. Most people use a combination of two or more of the above learning styles when attempting to learn new information.

Your goal as a preacher is to pass on to others the Word of God, but you must consider how to best communicate this to a diverse audience. If you don't and you only teach to one learning style, you may lose the attention of the other three-quarters of your congregation. A pastor who relies solely on PowerPoint with bulleted lists of information might keep the attention of a math teacher, but the speech pathologist might be writing out her grocery list. A service filled with theatrics, role-playing and music might captivate an artistic director but put an engineer to sleep. Youth leaders might fist pump when asked to turn to their neighbor to pray or discuss a question, but the artist might shrink into her seat and break into a sweat at the thought of having to speak with someone she doesn't know.

On top of that, your audience has a diverse set of personalities (or temperaments) that can affect how a person learns. Books upon books have been written to make sense of the different ways people are wired.

One profile, developed by Dr. Gary Smalley and Dr. John Trent, bases personalities and temperaments around animal characteristics—a simple and helpful way to identify personality types. Even a young child can understand this method!

Lion (Choleric/Dominant)

Strengths: Visionary, practical, productive, strong-willed, independent, decisive, leader.

Weaknesses: Cold, domineering, unemotional self-sufficient, unforgiving, sarcastic, cruel.

Otter (Sanguine/Influence)

Strengths—Outgoing, responsive, warm, friendly, talkative, enthusiastic, compassionate.

Weaknesses—Undisciplined, unproductive, exaggerates, egocentric, unstable.

Golden Retriever *(Phlegmatic/Steadiness)*

Strengths— Calm, easy-going, dependable, quiet, objective, diplomatic, humorous.

Weaknesses—Selfish, stingy, procrastinator, unmotivated, indecisive, fearful, worrier.

Beaver *(Melancholy/Compliance)*

Strengths— Analytical, self-disciplined, industrious, organized, aesthetic, sacrificing.

Weaknesses— Moody, self-centered, touchy, negative, unsociable, critical, revengeful.

Some pastors might preach in a way in which their voice grows progressively louder and louder, until it borders on yelling, just to make a point! But how will this go over with the Golden Retriever personality? You can almost pick these people out from the crowd when a pastor's voice grows loud and passionate.

Preaching from an organized outline thrills the Beaver, but bores the Otter, who would respond better to turning to a neighbor and sharing a life experience.

And don't forget the gender makeup of your audience. Chances are half of the people listening tune out to another football illustration. A single woman will likely grow frustrated with too many illustrations on marriage or parenting.

When planning your sermon, consider all of the different learning styles and personality types gathering on any given Sunday, and ask yourself:

- *Have I considered people's learning styles and temperaments when planning this message?*

- *Have I incorporated a variety of tools to help engage people —such as a skit, a formal outline, a video or a related song? Can I identify at least four of them in my sermon?*

- *Have I considered different genders, age brackets, and seasons of life?*

If you are at a loss for ideas for how to teach effectively to someone who learns visually, schedule coffee with an art teacher. If you need help engaging auditory learners, seek advice from your worship leaders.

When you preach, your own personality naturally comes forth. Just make sure you consider others' personality and temperaments as well. Again, if you are unsure, ask for help. If you have a Beaver personality, ask someone with an Otter personality for wisdom to reach more outgoing, talkative members of your church. The goal is to put yourself in someone else's shoes.

Now, with these various learning styles, personalities and temperaments in mind, consider the different questions that might surface in regards to your message. For example, a person who learns mathematically or logically might ask the question, *"What does this random skit have to do with the price of eggs?"*

Sermon Enhancers (With Different Learning Styles and Temperaments in Mind)

Here are some different ways to incorporate sermon "enhancers" into your message, with different learning styles and temperaments in mind:

- Ask a question or two that people can respond to. Ask for a show of hands, or walk down the aisle with a microphone, to solicit responses.

- Leave a piece of paper under the pews that includes a question or challenge.

- Leave cards randomly throughout the rows of chairs or pews, with something to read at home tied directly to the sermon.

- Invite the congregation to take two minutes to Tweet something, or to text somebody, as an immediate application of the message (others who are not technically inclined could use this time to jot down notes or talk quietly with another nearby).

- Challenge the congregation to think of names of people they need to seek out for forgiveness or restoration.

- Give your congregation a few minutes of silence during or after your message to pray or meditate on what you have just preached.

- Conduct live interviews with people a few weeks before a particular message and use the footage to craft a video to show during your message that makes a powerful point.

- Invite a member of the congregation who is a gifted dancer to perform during the service to a song with lyrics that tie in to the message.

- Pass out a small trinket to each person to help him or her remember the main point of the message.

The possibilities are endless! You'll never be able to teach to all of the different learning styles and personalities. But approaching your message with ideas like these in mind certainly results in better audience engagement.

Chapter Summary:

Undoubtedly, questions surface in your listener's mind—subconsciously or consciously—during your message. Your job is to anticipate what these questions are, and fashion your message in a way that answers them. Anticipate questions your audience doesn't even know they have, or questions that stem from different theological views, pain, or unclear words. Plan how to address those concerns. This settles our hearts and makes us feel seen, heard, and validated.

Consider different learning styles and personality temperaments as well when planning your sermons.

Once you have considered our questions, your next move is to make sure we understand what your sermon means for our lives, in great detail. In Chapter 7, I encourage you to *Show Us How*, the sixth pillar.

Take our survey at <u>SermonToBook.com</u> to see if your sermons are ready for a book!

Articulate Our Questions

Step into the shoes of the most diverse group of five members in your congregation. What questions are they asking about your sermon (even though they don't realize it yet)? Articulate these and make it your aim to find God's answer by your sermon's end. Next, look for points in your sermon where doctrinal/theological differences may come into play. How can you make members of your congregation feel understood and cared for? Work these into your sermon.

6—Show Us How

"We often belabor men with arguments and appeals, when they are much more in need of practical and simple explanations, as regards what to do, and how to do it." — **John A. Broadus, On the Preparation and Delivery of Sermons**

A BASKETBALL TEAM can get pulverized in the final quarter and still win. A football team can cough up the football, throw interceptions, and surrender numerous touchdowns in the last fifteen minutes and still obtain the victory.

But when it comes to the 100-meter dash, no matter how well the runner sprints through the first 90 meters, a simple stumble in the final 20 meters guarantees a devastating loss.

The same is true of the final moments of your sermon.

No matter how well you snatch our attention, simplify the point, help us see why, give us proof, and articulate our questions, your sermon will fizzle—much like a firework that appears majestic but emits a pathetic pop—if you leave us without a clear understanding of how we should practically apply the message to our daily lives.

This is why you must give us authentic, down-to-earth advice on how to practice what you've preached. James 1:22 says: "But be doers of the word, and not hearers only, deceiving yourselves." Keep this verse in mind as you bring your sermon to a close.

How Do I Create Actionable Items?

"The goal of application is to build a bridge from the Bible to today's listeners. This means we analyze the audience as carefully as the text." — **The Preacher's Complete Skills Guide, Christianity Today**

Most sermon applications won't take your audience by surprise. People intrinsically know where they fall short, even unbelievers. What they want to know is how to fix the problem, or how to close the gap between their transgressions and a place of peace.

Begin by asking yourself these seven questions, which helps you formulate clear action items:

- What is the main point of your message (i.e., your *Sermon Summary Sentence*)?

- How did the text you are preaching apply in the culture and context it was originally written?

- Who might be listening to your message?

- Does your text address different types of people?

- Does your text address the Body of Christ, the church?

- Can the gospel be preached from the passage you are preaching on?

- Does this passage help believers know God more intimately?

- What does the problem or need you are addressing in your message look like?

- What kind of response are you looking for, and what might be preventing your audience from responding this way?

- Can you suggest different steps your listeners can take to begin resolving the problem?

Now, let's look at each of these questions in more detail:

What is the main point of your message (i.e., your Sermon Summary Sentence)? The more accurately and precisely you nail your Sermon Summary Sentence at the beginning of the planning process, the better prepared you are to encourage personal application to your audience. So, your first step should be to write out your Sermon Summary Sentence (yes, again). You cannot hit a target with a crooked arrow, and you want these application points to cut right to your listeners' hearts.

How does the text you're using apply to the culture it was originally written for? As students of the Word, it is easy to interpret Scripture according to the culture and context we presently live in—where *we* live, who *we* hang around, and the uniqueness of *our* family unit. However, it is important to consider how the text applied to listeners in its original context. It may have been a command by God, a truth about God, or a warning of upcoming destruction.

Set the text in the context and culture it was written in, and then ask yourself: *Are theses truths or warnings timeless? Or were they written specifically for that generation?* Formulate your action items through this grid.

Jeramie Rinne, author of **Learning the Art of Sermon Application,** said if your application grows organically from the soil of your passage, it will ring true with your congregation. They will know that the Word of God itself, and not just the cleverness of the preacher, is pricking their hearts.

Does this text address different types of people? For example, does your text speak differently to believers than it does to unbelievers? Does it identify a particular group, such as mothers, children, Gentiles or religious leaders? Does your text provide implications for marriage, finances or happiness? Contrast God's Word with worldly approaches when creating application items for a powerful result.

Does this text address the Body of Christ as a whole? Step back and look at the text from a corporate, rather than an individual, perspective. Sometimes a text has profound meaning for the body of Christ as a whole. Considering this may result in tremendous application steps for growth in your church.

Does the text you are preaching lend itself to a clear presentation of the gospel? The gospel is the central, most important message of the Bible, and the most transformational action points often are birthed from this truth. Ask yourself where the gospel is in your text, where you see God's holiness and goodness displayed, or where God expressed His displeasure with sin.

Now it's time to actually write out some action items. Ask yourself these questions to spur on some ideas:

- What actionable items naturally flow out of your sermon?

- Do they avoid the sinful trench of legalism?

- Are *you* striving to live the way you're suggesting *we* live?

Write down at least one specific action you want the individuals in your congregation to take—or as many as come to mind (in order of importance). Show your congregation what it looks like to put your sermon into practice as they follow Jesus. It may be something like this:

> *"Identify one area of sin in your life that is keeping you in a place of bondage, and ask a trusted friend or spouse to hold you accountable to turning from that sin."*

Or

> *"Look for one way this week you can serve your spouse in humility, as Jesus serves you."*

Now, let's look at examples of some "super" actionable items.

Help Your Congregation With Super Actionable Items

Going back to the pastor who addressed a group of high school students about sexual purity (*Help Us See Why*), let's take a look at how he introduced super actionable items for staying physically unblemished.

First, the pastor set the stage by reminding the young people that there's a reason why God says to run from impurity (1 Corinthians 6:18); to put impurity to death (Colossians 3:5); to leave no room for the flesh to do what it wants (Romans 13:14); and that no person can carry fire and not get burned (Proverbs 6:27-28).

Second, he restated that purity isn't about not doing sinful things, but waiting for the *best* thing.

Then he got to the shoe leather, breaking down actionable items into bullet points that he expounded upon with short stories and clarifying points:

- Determine to date people who love Jesus and want His standard. Choose to be attracted to the Jesus you see in the opposite sex.

- Determine what you must do to keep yourself— and your significant other—pure when you're together (i.e. stay in public places instead of secluded settings).

- Recruit a support team of parents, mentors, and other people who love you and help you follow God's standard.

- Fill yourself with what is true, noble, just, and good. Because if you're feeding yourself with things that encourage lust, it comes easier to you in the relationship.

- Personal pledges of purity don't work—at least not for long. Instead create situations where you cannot sin against the other person.

- Be mindful of the alarms the Holy Spirit uses to warn you of danger, such as those times when your mind reels with the possibility of failure.

- Never roll the dice in your relationship (i.e. going a step further physically because you *think* you can handle it).

- Modesty matters, so be mindful of what you wear and ask yourself: *Am I keeping my significant other safe from lust?*

- What we say and how we say it matters, so ask yourself: *Do my words lift the other person's eyes to Jesus, or simply turn them on to me?*

Including action items in your message moves your audience toward living a new way in light of his or her change. If done properly, showing us how to apply your sermon should be the most difficult part of your sermon prep. Generalization is easy; being specific is difficult.

> *"The application in a sermon is not merely an appendage to the discussion, or a subordinate part of it, but is the main thing to be done."* — **John A. Broadus, On the Preparation and Delivery of Sermons**

Chapter Summary:

Showing us how to apply your sermon is an important and also difficult step. Take time to think through the original culture and context your text was written, the different types of people your text addresses, whether the text speaks to individuals or the corporate body of Christ, and whether the gospel can be pulled from the text. Considering the main point of your message spurs your thinking toward engaging actionable items.

After formulating your applications, it's time to write your conclusion. Chapter 8 challenges you to *Inspire Us to Go* (the seventh and final pillar)!

Take our survey at <u>SermonToBook.com</u> to see if your sermons are ready for a book!

Show Us How

What actionable items lend themselves to your sermon? Write down at least one specific action you want your congregation to take—or as many as you can think of (in order of importance). Show your congregation what it looks like to put your sermon into practice as they follow Jesus.

7—Inspire Us to Go

"It is not enough to convince men of truth, nor enough to make them see how it applies to themselves, and how it might be practicable for them to act it out—but we must 'persuade men.'" — ***John A. Broadus, On the Preparation and Delivery of Sermons***

THE SWORD OF AN IMPASSIONED soldier swings swifter than that of a soldier just doing his duty.

This is why the best leaders in history made it a priority to not only address their troops before war, but also tap into the raw aspects that made them human: love, courage, hope, sacrifice, honor.

As a pastor on Sunday mornings, you can either perspire and retire, or inspire and set on fire. The body of Christ desperately needs the latter.

How is this accomplished? It can only be done through depending on the Holy Spirit. But you must also remember that you're a vehicle through which the Spirit works, and that the way you choose to conclude your sermon matters tremendously. It is the final opportunity for the sermon to accomplish its intended purpose.

Avoiding Weak Conclusions

Before we look at techniques to writing a strong sermon conclusion, let's take a minute to consider some weak ones. Pastor Peter Mead leads the Preacher's Networks at the European Leadership Forum. He lists ten types of conclusions pastors should avoid when planning their sermons, to prevent messages from ending with a fizzle. We'll look at these finishes "Dave Letterman style," as the top ten ways *not* to wrap up your sermon.

10. **The "Not Again" Finish:** These conclusions are the same ones the pastor has used every week for as long as people can remember.

9. **The "Left Field" Finish:** These types of conclusions have little to do with the passage the pastor just preached on.

8. **The "Gospel-Out-Of-Nowhere" Finish:** This is where the preacher has left the gospel out of the central message, and tries to include it in the conclusion as a last chance attempt of transforming people.

7. **The "Overly-Emotional" Finish**: These conclusions attempt to fortify an emotional response from listeners by throwing in a random heart-tugging story at the very end. The congregation may end up feeling disconnected to the main points of the message and emotionally drained.

6. **The "Searching-For-a-Runway" Finish:** Here the preacher knows he needs to land the plane but is searching desperately for a runway on which to land it. As you are descending you remember that you haven't reinforced a particular point of the message, so you pull up and circle around for another attempt and your message drags on. (More on "landing the plane" later!)

5. **The "Discouraging Finale" Finish:** People need to leave your message encouraged, but these endings typically include a discouraging line or two that deflates your congregation. Finish your message on a hopeful, uplifting note.

4. **The "Uncomfortable Fade" Finish:** These awkward conclusions end with the pastor fishing for words that releases his audience from their seats. For example, he might stumble over the phrase, "Uh, that's all I have for you today." As soon as those words roll off your tongue, you've lost credibility with us.

3. **The "Machine Gun" Finish:** You've already given us action points in your message, but these conclusions fire off another round of random applications in hopes of hitting a bulls eye (which they rarely do). The conclusion is a good place to emphasize that we are to be doers of the Word (James 1:22), not to offer innovative ways to do it.

2. The "New Information" Finish: Avoid introducing any new information at the end of your message. Even a concluding story or last-chance illustration is risky.

And the number one weak sermon conclusion is…

1. The "Just Stop" Finish: These conclusions simply drop out of the sky. Suddenly the message is over, with no clear conclusion, and the audience is left scratching their heads.

You can avoid these pitfalls by planning out your conclusion before you even step up to the podium. I offer some ideas in a coming chapter, but for now, there are three basic steps to help you finish your sermon with a bang.

- **Review**: This part of your conclusion summarizes and informs, bringing together your message. Make sure this full picture always points back to Christ.

- **Encourage**: Encourage response to and application of the message. This is your call to action. It should challenge each listener to act on the information you have just reviewed.

- **Stop**: The conclusion has to include, at some point, a phenomenon known as "stopping." You need one conclusion, not three or four. The apostle Paul wrote "finally" seven times in Philippians, but you are not writing the book of Philippians. You are writing a conclusion.

Review. Encourage. Stop. If you do nothing else, abide by these three steps. You'll finish your message with confidence and an attentive audience.

Land the Plane

Too often pastors let their conclusions drag on and on. Don't keep circling the airport; land the aircraft and head for the gate. Pastor Mead writes:

"Passengers who have had a great journey with a bad landing will leave with their focus entirely on the bad landing. Passengers want the pilot to know where he is going and to take them straight there. They don't particularly want the pilot to finish a normal journey with a historic televised adrenaline landing. Passengers like a smooth landing, but they'll generally take a slight bump over repeated attempts to find the perfect one. Once landed, extended taxiing is not appreciated. A good landing that takes you by surprise always seems to have a pleasant effect."

A sermon is like a love affair—it's easier to start one than to end one. But if it never ends, it might only get worse!

Ideas for Conclusions

Just like fish don't always like the same bait—sometimes it's a worm and sometimes it's a fly—your conclusion should make use of whatever catches the most fish. It has been said that the goal of the conclusion should be to "storm the citadel of the will and capture it for Jesus Christ." Vary your techniques, to "catch" people for Christ.

Below are some very simple tactics for doing this through your conclusion.

- **Argument**: Anticipate any objections your audience may have and logically refute them.

- **Warning**: Alert your audience of the consequences of disobedience.

- **Compassion**: Express God's love and concern for them and others.

- **Vision**: Paint a picture of what is possible if your listeners obey God. Help them live their faith.

- **Encouragement**: Spur your audience on; they can do anything through Christ who strengthens them.

- **Personal Touch**: Your audience should feel like you are talking one-on-one with each of them.

- **Piercing Question:** Engage people by helping them process and apply the message.

- **Surprise**: Powerful conclusions sometimes sneak up on congregations rather than being blatant and expected.

Before you write your conclusion, ask yourself the following questions:

- What is my Sermon Summary Sentence (again)?

- What are the major points I have made in my sermon, and how can I restate them without repeating them word for word?

- Is there an appropriate argument, warning, encouraging word, or piercing question I can use in my conclusion to support these points?

Then, consider filtering your sermon's conclusion through these four points:

Your sermon fully realized: What would the global church look like in six months if every member took you message to heart and applied it to their lives? What would your message, fully realized and acted upon, transform in *your* congregation? What would change? Whose lives would be impacted? Where would transformation happen? Answer these questions and cast the vision to us.

Help them fight their flesh: Your vision-cast represents a pristine scenario. But it's only the start of your conclusion because our lives, struggles, and motives are not pristine. We need you to get in the trenches with us and encourage us in our daily battle against the flesh.

How can you meet us in our humanity as you inspire us toward the vision? How can you dive deep into our weakness to simultaneously draw out our strength? How can you show us that we're in this together and need each other for the journey? Look for the fleshly roadblocks we face as we start our week, and show us why we can overcome those roadblocks: *Jesus Christ.*

Ask open-ended questions: Martyn Lloyd-Jones concluded his sermon, "The Breadth, Length, Depth, and Height of God's Love" with a series of open-ended questions, such as:

"Have you been feeling sorry for yourself, and somewhat lethargic in a spiritual sense? Have you been regarding worship and prayer as tasks? Have you allowed the world, the flesh, or the devil to defeat you and to depress you? The one antidote to that is to meditate upon and to contemplate this love of Christ. Have you realized its breadth, its length, its depth, and its height? Have you realized who and what you are as a Christian? Have you realized that Jesus is 'the Lover of your soul', that He has set His affection upon you? Have you realized the height of His ambition for you? 'Child of God, shouldst thou repine'? Are we but to shuffle through this world?"

It's not surprising that this sermon has gone on to become one of the most powerful sermons in history. It cuts straight to the areas of life that most people struggle with. Open-ended questions engage our minds and hearts. They help set the table for us to hear and respond to the Spirit of God. What open-ended questions can you ask that accomplish the same?

Speak to numerous walks of life: In his sermon, "Christ's Greatest Trophy," J.C. Ryle concluded with the following statements (which he expounded upon):

"This message may fall into the hands of some humble–hearted and contrite sinner. Are you that man? Then here is encouragement for you...

"This message may fall into the hands of some proud and presumptuous man of the world. Are you that man? Then take warning...

"This message may fall into the hands of someone who is mourning over departed believers. Are you such a one? Then take comfort from this Scripture...

"And this message may fall into the hands of some aged servant of Christ. Are you such a one? Then see from these verses how near you are to home..."

Take this approach to heart. We come in all shapes and sizes—in spiritual maturity, season of life, and hardships suffered. Do your best to think through the different lives represented in your pews and speak directly not only to one, but to as many as you can.

The Power of Circularity

Great storytellers, directors, comedians and writers use what is called "Circularity." This is where something at the beginning of a story, play or book is left intentionally hanging that can be brought full circle at the end.

Ask yourself if there is anything in your message you can bring full circle:

- Was there a point that wasn't quite finished?

- Can you revisit a story and retell it in a way that brings a final "aha!" to your message?

- Did you use a quote at the beginning of your message that could be spoken again to make a powerful concluding statement?

An Impassioned Response Is Not Far Away

"Do you want to make an impression or do you want to make an impact? It's great to hear, 'good message!' Yet, it's better when a person's life is impacted with the gospel and it brings about lasting life-change." — Vanable Moody II

Each person in your congregation most likely responds your sermon in one of two ways. They either look at it as a nicely presented exposition to which they nod in approval. Or they fall to their to their knees, hearts bleeding with love, adoration, and a desperate desire to serve Jesus Christ and build His Kingdom.

The first response is pride and apathy; the second is humility and action.

"Appeal to the individual for a response," says Charles W. Koller in *How to Preach Without Notes*. "Either an action or a resolve, a pledge of dedication or rededication to Christ at some clear point, or a response of thanksgiving."

Will every text lend itself to an impassioned response? No. But always remember that if every sermon ultimately points to Jesus—and every sermon should—then an impassioned response is not far away. You simply have to dig deep to find it, experience it, and preach it.

Don't rush through your conclusion. Instead, bring it to a fiery focus that's clear, compelling, and climactic. Don't falsely excite feelings, but genuinely arouse the people of God to live like children who are loved, freed, and sent on the grandest mission this world has ever known.

No matter what, approach your conclusion with the goal of gripping our hearts. You've informed our minds, and now you must awaken our emotions and challenge our resolve. Your conclusion should be the emotional high point of the sermon. Think of your conclusion as a lawyer's concluding argument. The lawyer knows that no matter how eloquently he argues his case, if his closing arguments don't draw forth a positive verdict, he has failed. Your audience should feel like the message is complete, they are on your side, and they are ready to take on the world.

"I preach as though Christ were crucified yesterday, rose from the dead today, and is coming back to earth again tomorrow!" — **Martin Luther**

Chapter Summary:

Your conclusion is an important part—if not the most important part—of your message. As amazing and powerful as your sermon might have been, if your conclusion is lackluster, your audience may leave thinking the entire message was, too. Avoid conclusions that are weak or never-ending, or leave your audience confused or frustrated. Instead, review your key points, encourage your audience, and then stop. There is no need to ramble on or add new information. Grip our hearts, and then close your mouth!

You've just finished the seventh structural pillar! You now have everything at your fingertips to write a powerful sermon that will greatly impact your congregation. If you're like most pastors, though, you're probably thinking, "I would love to apply the seven pillars to my sermon prep, but where am I going to find the time?" In Chapter 9, I help you *Take Control of Your Week.*

Take our survey at SermonToBook.com to see if your sermons are ready for a book!

Inspire Us To Go

Write a passionate appeal to love Jesus Christ from the depths of the human soul, to love others as He loves, and to make disciples of all nations. What would your sermon, fully realized and applied, mean to the world? How can you encourage your congregation through their daily battles against the flesh? Try putting together a series of pointed, practical questions that are tied to your sermon. And finally, think through what your sermon means to different people/ages in your flock, and list them accordingly.

Take Control of Your Week

"If you don't know where you are going, you are going to end up somewhere else." — ***Anonymous***

EVERY PASTOR HAS TWO SUNDAYS IN THE WEEK: the one he is getting over, and the one that arrives six days later. It is important to take steps to order your week to prevent your responsibilities on these two Sundays from adding unnecessary stress on the days between. No pastor wants to be worrying on Friday or Saturday what to say on Sunday!

If you are not by nature a disciplined person, you will need to be aggressive about scheduling time into your week for prayer, study, and planning for your sermon.

Stephen Covey, the well-known author of *The 7 Habits of Highly Effective People*, says, "The key is not to prioritize what is on your schedule, but to schedule your priorities." Though family and the needs of the church *should* be at the top of your list of priorities, those responsibilities can make it difficult to carve out time for your sermon. On the contrary, if you are not disciplined in prepping your sermon efficiently, it can eat up too much time to the neglect of your family and the body of Christ. Develop a system that works for you, and then do everything in your power to maintain it. Here are some ideas for how to do this:

Schedule time each day when you are not available by phone. If you are a morning person, block your time from say 8:00-11:30 a.m. If you work better in the afternoon, plan your day around that block of time. Let your wife or administrative assistant take calls for you. Close your office door, turn your mobile phone off, and put your to-do list aside.

Block off an entire day each week. Another method is to block off an entire day at the beginning of the week for sermon preparation. On this day, make yourself unavailable for meetings, calls or pastoral duties. Do not allow the affairs of the church to interfere with this time. If you have an assistant, make them the gatekeeper. Their job is to deflect anything that comes up away from you. Make it clear what emergencies you are willing to be interrupted for, and what things you are not.

Schedule non-negotiable meetings. In 1 Peter 5:2-4, Peter says pastors are to care for God's flock with a willing heart and as an example for others. The book of Hebrews says the pastor will give an account for souls (Hebrews 13:17). Because of this high calling, and because much of what you do with your flock may *not* constitute the caring for their souls, be deliberate about making time for this by scheduling non-negotiable meetings. These meetings should be solely to tend to the people God has given you to care for: the widows, those who are grieving, those who are sick, those who are weak, and every other person in your congregation under your care. This is the pastor's true calling, and it should never be pushed aside or delegated solely to others' to-do lists. Your sermon preparation should revolve around this calling.

After you've cataloged your first two or three non-negotiable meetings for the week, there will not be many other windows of time available for other meetings or administration. You may need to solicit help for additional discipleship or for planning meetings, counseling, or visits and care for other church members.

Schedule necessary church administration. The pastor is not required to take care of *all* of his church's administrative needs, but some require his attention. Discern what administrative tasks you need to complete, and what can be delegated to someone else who is not responsible to preach. Delegating this responsibility helps assure the church runs in a smooth and well-organized manner (1 Peter 5:2). Delegating will also give you more time to focus on your first three priorities: your family, shepherding your people, and preparing your message.

Your flock always includes sheep with a long list of needs, and unfortunately many go unmet. Minister where you can, delegate where you cannot and trust God for the rest.

> *"Therefore, my dear brothers and sisters, stand firm.*
> *Let nothing move you. Always give yourselves fully to*
> *the work of the Lord, because you know that your labor*
> *in the Lord is not in vain."* — **1 Corinthians 15:58, NIV**

Depend upon God alone as you press on in what you are called to do; your hard work is not in vain (and it's not going unseen).

Paul wrote to his disciple Timothy that part of preaching the word is to be prepared for the work:

> *"In the presence of God and of Christ Jesus, who will judge the living and the dead, and in view of his appearing and his kingdom, I give you this charge: Preach the word; be prepared in season and out of season; correct, rebuke and encourage—with great patience and careful instruction."* — **2 Timothy 2:1-2**

Paul's message to pastors rings true even more so today. You must be prepared in all seasons. You are called to instruct us carefully, correct, rebuke and encourage us. Without adequate preparation, your messages simply won't accomplish these things, and be all they can be (or all God *intends* them to be).

Create a Sermon Calendar

"A preacher has to be like a squirrel and collect and store matter for the future days of winter." — **D. Martin Lloyd Jones, Preaching and Preachers**

Annual sermon planning can greatly improve the quality of your preaching. At first, this statement might seem like an oxymoron; *how can a pastor plan for a message six months out?*

There are different ways to develop a *Sermon Calendar*, either for the year, the quarter or even the month. You don't need to come up with every detail for your messages, only the general topics. Doing so is paramount when you approach your sermon planning for the week. You will have already decided on your topic months prior. And by this time, you'll likely already have your simplified point in mind, stories to pull from, and proof for your message.

I recommend creating a *Sermon Calendar* for the year because doing so helps you plan other church programs around your sermon schedule. But there are some other benefits as well:

- Service opportunities that coincide with your sermon topics can be established.

- Bible Study groups centered on your messages can be created.

- Sermon illustrations can be found and filed months in advance.

- Personal weekends away can be easily scheduled.

- Guest speakers or preachers can be considered and invited in plenty of time for a particular weekend.

Consider scheduling a planning retreat by yourself, for the purpose of seeking God's wisdom for your upcoming messages. This is where many pastors come up with a framework for sermon topics. If retreating for a few days is not an option, schedule out a specific time during your regular schedule to create your *Sermon Calendar* for the month, quarter or year.

Calendaring your sermons should not be treated like an item to check off your to-do list. You are a messenger of the Most High God—an ambassador of the Lord Jesus Christ, a herald of the greatest story ever told and the best news ever received (2 Corinthians 5:20; 1 Corinthians 15:1-4). Therefore, planning your sermons should not be done flippantly.

Above all, filter your planning time through the grid of prayer. As you pray, ask God:

- *What truths He wants you to teach His people this year.*

- *What the spiritual condition is of the people He has given you to shepherd.*

- *What His vision is for your church.*

- *If there is a weakness in the congregation that needs to be addressed.*

- *What cultural challenges people are struggling with. Is there an election on the horizon? An economic issue?*

Your topics, and any sermon series, should flow from these questions. Mapping out where you want (where *God* wants) to take your congregation is vital.

Then, you review (and review and review) this calendar throughout the year, and possibly discard certain messages as God leads. Remember, as much as you plan, the Holy Spirit is ultimately in charge.

"The mind of man plans his way, But the LORD directs his steps." — **Proverbs 16:9**

If God nudges you to put aside a message to teach on something else one week, don't be afraid to do it. Your Sermon Calendar is meant to give you a clear destination, but with flexibility to deviate down a different road.

In his book *Preaching: Simple Teaching on Simply Preaching*, Alec Motyer reminds pastors that sermons are not spontaneous or extended intuitions but things to be worked at. Just like grass doesn't remain green from an occasional heavy watering but needs regular tending, so too are sermons. Regularly tending to them—thinking on them well before you preach them—brings positive results.

Rob Hurtgen, pastor of First Baptist Church in Chillicothe, Missouri, offers this list of ideas to consider including on your Sermon Calendar:

- ***Preaching dates.*** For most churches, these will be Sundays.

- *Holiday dates.* When is Easter? Mothers Day? Christmas? Is your church celebrating an anniversary? Confirm which of these special calendar dates your church recognizes and if your message should center on this holiday. For example, will you teach about the resurrection on Easter? Will you address parenting on Mother or Father's day?

- *Non-religious dates.* Include specific days that aren't religious at all, like Super Bowl Sunday, Labor Day or the first day of school for your district. These dates impact when you might begin or end a particular sermon series, and help you make the most of your congregation's natural seasonal patterns.

- *Scripture texts.* If you already know the main Scripture for a certain message or sermon series, enter it on your calendar.

- *Prayerfully choose themes.* Some pastors repeat certain topics every year, such as the mission of the church in the summer, or marriage and parenting in the fall, or spiritual disciplines in the winter. If you have some hard themes, leave space for them on the calendar. When praying about and planning for these things, ask yourself how they naturally incorporate into the various ministries in your church.

- ***Consider the season when planning your sermons and sermon series.*** Autumn is typically the time when people settle down and make new commitments to Bible Studies and volunteering in church ministry. By May or June that spark of energy that fueled them in the fall is often waning (or gone). Mentally, many people in your congregation are preparing for summer break—and sadly, this includes a break from deep topics at church. Consider this when calendaring.

- ***Central theme of the message.*** Do the hard work of determining the primary point of the sermon text when you are calendaring. You may be planning a series that connects ideas together, but you should still be able to identify the central theme of your text for each sermon.

- ***Biblical genre.*** To ensure the whole counsel of God is preached (rather than just your favorite book), this column reminds you of genres you have already touched on.

- ***Additional notes.*** Document other items you want to remember that may affect the order of service and the sermon. Consider special holidays or community activities that may coincide with your sermon.

Once you have developed the framework of your *Sermon Calendar*, reflect on other details that may affect the flow of your sermons. Ask yourself these questions and make adjustments as necessary:

- *When will I take a vacation?*

- *Do I want to leave gaps between a sermon series to fill in with stand-alone topics?*

- *When do I expect to invite guest preachers? When will I need to?*

Regardless of all your other responsibilities as a preacher, everything centers on the weekly sermon you deliver. You lead us better, and are more confident and compassionate when handling God's Word, by utilizing a *Sermon Calendar*. The more disciplined you are in planning ahead—the more we trust you!

There is an old adage that says, "When you fail to plan, you plan to fail." Planning for the future may feel like a fifty-pound weight around your neck, but think of sermon planning as an investment. The resulting dividends are worth the initial time and effort you put in to the message.

A *Sermon Calendar* saves valuable time in the long run when you begin detailing out each sermon. When the time comes to craft a certain message, your resources will be close at hand in the filing system you've created. And each message will have been in the back of your mind for some time. No doubt you'll already have a pretty good idea of where you want to go.

A *Sermon Calendar* also reduces stress. And it ensures a variety of different topics are addressed throughout the year because everything is well organized and thought out. It keeps your church on a very clear and organized path.

Ultimately, creating a *Sermon Calendar* gives you freedom. Having a plan that you can invite the Holy Spirit to affirm or redirect is far more effective than having no plan at all.

Invite Others Into the Planning Process

"We all serve each other. The way I serve our Creative Team, Worship Team and the Video Team, is try my best to plan as far ahead as possible...then everybody can give their best effort possible. They don't serve me; we serve each other." — **Perry Noble, Senior Pastor Newspring Church**

Once you've spent time seeking the Lord and mapping out multiple sermons, it's time to share your *Sermon Calendar* with your staff (i.e. board members, the church receptionist, worship team leaders, the graphic designer, the outreach coordinator, etc.). This is the exciting part of the planning process. Now, the church as a whole can become invested in where the Spirit has led you in your sermon prep.

Here are a few practical benefits that happen when you share your *Sermon Calendar* with your staff:

- Your worship leaders are able to select songs based on topics or themes you've already mapped out.

- Your aesthetics team is able to plan for décor accordingly.

- Your communications and/or graphics team is blessed by knowing the theme in plenty of time to create Powerpoint slides, program inserts and marketing pieces that connect to your sermon.

- The church's social media outlets can be in sync.

Benefits for Creating and Sharing Your *Sermon Calendar*

It focuses the entire church on the same vision. Your ministry leaders catch the buzz and, in turn, excite members of the congregation as certain messages approach. This builds everyone's anticipation for the upcoming series.

It allows pastors to objectively review the coming year's sermons for variety and breadth. When a preacher covers the same topics over and over, his messages risk sounding stale or imbalanced. Planning keeps the pastor's messages fresh. It also allows pastors to delegate tasks they wouldn't otherwise have had time to delegate.

It creates evangelistic opportunities. When church leaders and members know what messages are on the horizon, they are able to invite friends and family members based on a very specific need or message.

The Importance of Theme

Post-modern church attendees respond well to themes. Preaching for four weeks on the book of Leviticus might produce some yawns; however, by repackaging the sermon series with the theme of "How to Draw Near to God" will most likely pique the interest of both longtime churchgoers and not-yet-believers.

Present your sermon series theme to your staff, so that their creative juices can begin flowing months before the sermon is even printed in the weekly program.

Your Preaching Team

Five amateur basketball players can accomplish more on the court working together as a team than playing as individuals. In the same way, when a church works together, the ripple effect reaches far more people for Christ than when the pastor tries to do everything himself. There is simply far too much for one pastor to juggle by himself. This is why gathering a preaching team not only blesses you by removing unnecessary responsibility and resulting stress, but it also impacts everyone involved.

Identify who this team is, and personally invite members to participate in the planning process. Seek their opinions prior to creating your annual calendar, and check in with them during the months before you speak on certain topics.

One option is to ask a few other leaders to read books you won't be able to get to. Instruct them to highlight key points, possible illustrations, or fresh interpretation on a subject or piece of Scripture. In this way, you glean from the best parts of the book without having to read the entire thing.

Pastor Perry Noble writes, "Invite the right people to lunch and tell them you want them to help you put your sermon together. They will come."

Creating a *Sermon Calendar*, inviting others into the planning process and forming a preaching team are simple action items that result in the removal of many things spilling off your plate of responsibilities. Though these suggestions may seem small, they keep your schedule balanced and reduce the possibility of physical or mental collapse because of overwork or stress.

Avoiding Burnout

"It boils down to this: I must have a balanced schedule, a healthy body, healthy relationships, the courage to be obedient to God no matter what he requires and most of all, a pure heart before God." — **Charles Stanley**

Burnout is the number one reason pastors leave the ministry. The possibility of burnout is very real and threatening to not only the pastor, but to his family and congregation.

To avoid burnout, start by never comparing yourself to other pastors or leaders. Paul was Paul; Peter was Peter; Apollos was Apollos. Each person is uniquely created and gifted for the ministry God called him to. Whether your church is a mega-church or a small gathering in a home, never second-guess the calling God has placed on your life because of how your ministry compares to the pastor down the street.

Tips To Prevent Burn-Out

Cultivate a dependence upon God. Everything you do should be grounded on a complete and utter dependence upon God. If you are depending on others or yourself for the work of the ministry, your focus is in the wrong place.

Lower your expectations. You are not the Lone Ranger; don't try to be! Delegate responsibility where appropriate, and trust other leaders to carry some of the weight that is dragging you down. Falling into the trap of thinking you can do it all is actually an inverted form of pride; vigorously guard against this!

Schedule rest and relaxation. Get a credit card that earns air miles and save them specifically for trips to recuperate. Schedule a day off here or there to work on projects around the house. Prioritize date nights with your wife, or dinners with friends. You must carve out time to refresh and reboot your system—or it will crash.

Seek fellowship from other pastors. No one can understand a pastor better than another pastor. Share your successes, trials and challenges. Guard against the lie that you have to protect your turf or your reputation, which leads to isolation.

Don't be someone you're not. After Saul dressed David with his armor, preparing him to fight the giant Goliath, David removed the armor and fought with nothing but his staff and five smooth stones (1 Samuel 17:38-40). David knew where his strength was based, and it was not in anything external.

Get help if you need it. One of the best things you can do for yourself, your family and your ministry may be to seek counseling. Don't let pride get in the way of your health. Those who are in the "helping" profession, of which pastors fall, face the highest risk of burnout.

Prioritize your marriage. It is not uncommon for marriages to suffer at the expense of ministry. You are pastor of your home before pastor of your congregation. Keeping your marriage healthy spills over into your ministry, and help prevent burnout.

Love Jesus more than the work of the gospel. This requires asking yourself a tough question: *Do I love what I do more than I love Jesus?* A good indicator of this is how much time you spend with God, reading and meditating on His Word, and communicating with Him in prayer compared to the amount of time you spend preparing your messages.

How Do I know If I'm Headed for Burnout?

Ask yourself the following questions. If your answer is "yes" to more than one, you may be burnt out or quickly headed there:

- Are you finding yourself getting angry quickly, irritated over minor issues, or overly defensive?

- Do you want to quit, or have you considered it more than once?

- Are you uptight around your spouse for no apparent reason?

- Do good friends irritate you?

- Are you finding yourself flying by the seat of your pants each week, with no desire to adequately prepare?

Don't avoid these obvious signs of exhaustion, anxiety and ultimately burnout. Swallow your pride, ask for help and seek counseling if necessary.

> *"Rather than ducking burnout like a prizefighter who is getting pummeled by his opponent, I think we should go on the offensive. With purpose, let's pursue the things that help us to conquer burnout before it conquers us!"* — **Rick Whitter**

Where Does the Holy Spirit Fit In?

Let's look again at the *Sermon Calendar*, which can really help prevent burnout. Some pastors are reluctant to use one for fear they might push out the work and leading of the Holy Spirit. However, Pastor Hurton writes:

> *"If you believe the Spirit leads, teaches and presses you into the future, you will see His leadership as assembling your entire preaching process. Countless*

times a sermon scheduled months in advance has spoken precisely to the issues men and women in the church were facing the day it was preached — even regarding newly emerging issues."

A *Sermon Calendar* won't limit the Holy Spirit. Rather, it places you in the position of deeper dependence on Him for what's ahead.

As I noted at the beginning of this chapter, every pastor has two Sundays in the week: the one he is getting over, and the one that arrives six days later. Planning ahead allows you to prepare for both and remove any looming anxiety about what you're going to preach each week.

Most importantly, planning well guards against sermon preparation time spilling over into your marriage. Don't make your ministry your mistress, (Ephesians 5:25). Always ask yourself, "Am I meeting my wife's needs?"

In addition to your husband responsibilities, spend quality time with your children. Being a pastor does not reduce your role as husband and father to third or fourth place (Ephesians 6:4). You are a child of God first, a husband and father second and a preacher third. Your children should grow to love the church, rather than hate it for taking their daddy (Brandon Hilgermann, *Preaching Nuts and Bolts: The essential Guide to Better Preaching*).

Chapter Summary:

Only you can take control of your week. If you do, your preaching becomes much more manageable, enjoyable and likely more powerful. You must be diligent about scheduling everything in your life, most importantly, your messages. The *Sermon Calendar* is an invaluable tool to help you do this. Creating a *Sermon Calendar* also benefits other ministries in your church, and bless your family as well. The end result? You lead with excellence the flock God has called you to shepherd.

Next, I address a sensitive subject that is inevitable for pastors: criticism. Though you are a mighty man of God commissioned for ministry, not everyone will be a fan of you or your preaching. Chapter 10 suggests some practical tips for *Responding to Sermon Criticism.*

Take our survey at SermonToBook.com to see if your sermons are ready for a book!

Take Control of Your Week

Schedule either one day, or a certain time every day that to pray about and plan for your upcoming sermon. Also schedule one or two full days to plan for the upcoming month, quarter or year. If possible, go away to somewhere private—even a hotel—to seek the Lord's direction for what He wants communicated for the upcoming moths. Commit to making it a habit to look for sermon illustrations all the time, based off your Sermon Calendar, not just the week you need them!

Respond to Sermon Criticism

"Criticism is the manure in which the Lord's servants grow best." — **Bishop Stephen Neill**

Regardless of how hard you work to implement the seven pillars in this book and create a calendar to produce the best sermons possible, you will receive criticism from someone. And though you might have a tough skin, nobody is made of Teflon. Criticism simply *hurts*.

Well, first of all, know that you are not alone! Even ancient biblical heroes endured criticism. David experienced horrible criticism and attack from his enemies. Agrippa, Festus, and other Jewish accusers criticized Paul (Acts 26). The Israelite's criticized Moses' leadership; Moses cried out to God, "What am I to do with these people? *They are almost ready to stone me*" (Exodus 17:4). Jesus, too, endured insults and misunderstandings. The Pharisees even accused Jesus of being Beelzebub—the son of the devil!

There are four questions you should ask yourself before dealing with the person who has shot the critical arrow into your heart:

Is the criticism valid? Though it might be hurtful, the criticism might be deserved. (However, there is a difference between constructive criticism and destructive (or even slanderous) criticism).

Am I doing my best with the life God has given me? You are only as good as what God allows you to be. Make sure you depend on God not only for your messages, but also your ability to deal with negativity. Stand firm in the truth of God's Word, seeking excellence in everything you do.

Am I willing to carry the cross of criticism for Christ's sake? Following Jesus makes you a walking target. Stephen was stoned to death for his convictions. Are you willing to face criticism for the sake of your Lord?

Am I guilty of criticizing others? Pastors are human and have the capability of criticizing just as much as the person listening to his message.

After asking yourself these questions, ask the Lord for the ability to think objectively about matters and the influence to help others do the same. Ask Him to help you react in a calm and loving way.

How To Respond

Criticism is inevitable. More often than not, it isn't valid. Sometimes, it is. Either way, there are godly, biblical ways to respond:

> ***Do not react with anger or vengeance.*** Wise King Solomon wrote, "A gentle answer turns away wrath, but a harsh word stirs up anger" (Proverbs 15:1). Give God space to use each criticism to transform you into a more godly person. Pray as Augustine prayed: "Lord, deliver me from the lust of vindicating myself!"

> ***Ask for forgiveness for any misunderstanding.*** If the person offended is not willing to forgive, it becomes their issue.

> ***Be open and honest with those who are doing the criticizing.*** Ask them for patience. Remind them that God is working on you (just as much as he is working on them).

> ***Defer or delay your response.*** Hold off speaking to the person who is upset with you to avoid confrontation, especially if you are sensing your emotions are boiling over. Spend time with the Lord, and cover yourself in prayer before approaching the critic.

> ***Avoid arguments.*** Paul wrote to Timothy, "Don't have anything to do with foolish and stupid arguments because you know they produce quarrels. The Lord's

servant must not quarrel; instead, he must be kind to everyone, able to teach, not resentful. Those who oppose him must gently instruct, in the hope that God will grant them repentance leading them to a knowledge of the truth" (2 Timothy 2:24-26).

Let the Holy Spirit change your critic's thinking. Even if the one criticizing does not alter his opinion or remains angry, God can do a work in his or her heart. Trust Him for the work you cannot see taking place.

Ask the Lord to help you learn something from every criticism. James tells us the trials of our faith produce endurance (James 1:1-6). In fact, James says it is these trials that bring maturity in Christ. Allow God to refine your character through criticism, knowing each time is maturing your faith.

Resist the temptation to take on new responsibilities or problems. Just because someone presents an issue or problem does not mean you need to add finding a solution to that problem to your to-do list. Perhaps it is the critic's responsibility to solve the problem!

Complaints often originate from other heart issues. Greed, envy, jealousy, anger, hatred, immaturity, ungodliness, rebelliousness, misunderstanding, presumption, lack of knowledge, lack of wisdom, or carnality can birth all kinds of muck in a person's heart.

Knowing this, pray for the character of the person complaining.

Encourage people to turn to God for the answers to their problems, questions, and complaints. Sometimes, you simply cannot say anything to rectify the situation. Remind your critic of the only One who can. Pray with them about the situation so that they know you care, but clearly communicate that only God has the solution.

Exhibit the qualities of 1 Corinthians 13:4-7. Above all, respond with patience and kindness. Do not be envious, do not boast, and guard against pride. Do not dishonor the person who is criticizing you, and do not respond in a self-seeking manner. Keep yourself from anger, and do not store up a record of wrongs against you. Rejoice in the truth of God's Word, and do everything to protect your brother and sister in Christ.

Ultimately, some complaints are like moldy food in the fridge; they just need to be thrown out. There is nothing you can do, so move on.

John A. Huffman, Jr., writes this about the criticism evangelist Billy Graham endured during his ministry:

"Billy Graham, over the decades, has been subject to the most intense criticism a man can face. Some claim he has violated the gospel of Jesus Christ by associating with ministers and laymen who deny the authority of the Bible

[handwritten: even Billy Graham was criticized]

and the deity of Christ. And there are those who attack him from the other side and say that he has neglected social concerns as he's put the stress on personal salvation. Some attack him for using the mass media and question his right to use Madison Avenue techniques. Some criticized him for going to Russia 20-something years ago. Even President Reagan publicly declared him as being used by the Soviet authorities. Billy Graham could spend many a sleepless night if he took all these criticisms too seriously."

Though some may have disagreed with his methods, nobody can argue Graham loved Jesus and impacted people for the kingdom. Billy Graham did not let differing opinions stop him from doing what God called him to do.

Responding to Sermon Criticism

Prepare a few answers ahead of time to respond to an upset member of your congregation. Practice them in front of a mirror. Then, when criticism hits, you are prepared with a loving response.

Responding by Letter or Email

Sometimes it may be appropriate to follow up a conversation with a critic with a letter or email. In my book *Pastor Email Power: 72 Letter Prompts That Help You Write A Perfect Note Even When You Don't Know What To Say,* I offer a template to help pastors respond to a critical congregant: (see template below)

Greet him/her. How would a shepherd greet his sheep? Greet your congregation in a way that displays care and love.

Connect at the heart level. Be transparent. Acknowledge you are not perfect. Avoid getting on the defensive. What ways have you seen your own fallen nature in your time as a pastor?

Step into his/her shoes. Acknowledge the specific criticisms that you are receiving. How can you imagine and relate to their feelings? How can you communicate that you care about their thoughts and opinions?

Meet his/her needs. Was there a misunderstanding? Is there information that would help clarify the issue? Without being defensive, explain your reasoning and support (if you feel you are in the right). If you are in the wrong, though, what do you need to repent of and seek forgiveness for?

Send him/her off with hope. Reaffirm your commitment to shepherd your congregation through thick and thin. What can you commit to doing to earn their trust again?

Again, however you respond, always do so in love. There is, according to Paul, no "more excellent way" (1 Cor. 12:31).

Chapter Summary:

Pastors inevitably face criticism. It's almost part of the job description. However, it is important to respond in a godly way that models the love of Christ to the one criticizing. Examine your own heart first to see if there is "any offensive way" in you (Psalm 139:23-24). Then, consider ways to respond that reflect the heart of God, build the other person up, and deflect arguments. If appropriate, send an email or handwritten letter to either address the situation or to follow up.

Now, I'd like to offer some suggestions to help refine your message before you preach it on Sunday. Chapter 11 helps you *Refine Your Message in One Cup of Coffee.*

Take our survey at <u>SermonToBook.com</u> to see if your sermons are ready for a book!

Refine Your Sermon Over A Cup of Coffee

LOOK AROUND YOU. Everything changes. Everything on this earth is in a continuous state of evolving, refining, improving, adapting, enhancing—changing (Steve Maraboli, *Life, the Truth, and Being Free*).

This includes your sermon.

Once you have worked through the 7 pillars and have created a solid message to share with your congregation, it's time to refine it.

Consider reviewing it with a trusted friend who is not shy about critiquing you. It doesn't have to be a long meeting. It can be over a one-hour cup of coffee.

Share a "miniature" version of your sermon by going to sermontobook.com and printing out the Template Guide and Template. It is as simple as filling in the blanks and printing off your notes. (NOTE: You will need to explain to your friend the 7 structural pillars we have talked about in this book so that he'll understand the different elements you want to make sure to include in your message).

Though it might seem awkward or "less spiritual" than giving your message on Sunday, Pastor Nicholas McDonald says practicing your sermon is actually an act of love toward those who hear it on Sunday morning.

Below are seven benefits McDonald offers for practicing your sermon ahead of time:

1. It helps illuminate your main point.

2. It shaves off wasted time. The first time you give your message out loud, it is usually ten minutes longer than the second time. Practicing helps make the message fluid.

3. It helps make connections clearer. Speaking your sermon helps you see where things need clarification, or where you may need stronger transitional sentences. Don't expect your congregation to move logically and smoothly from one point to another for you! Clear transitions enable your listeners to "see" the framework upon which you have built your thinking. You may have some bridgework to do if you stop or trip up after each point.

4. It gives you a sense of your sermon's drama. You won't be able to tell whether your sermon is captivating when it's on paper. After verbalizing it, you can shift things around to make your message flow more dramatically.

5. It shapes the way you say what you say. Some things read better on paper than they sound in reality. "Hearing" your message helps you know where to rephrase things to capture the point you are trying to make clearly and memorably.

6. It helps you from relying too heavily on notes on Sunday morning. Just as the planning process begins implanting the message in your head, speaking it solidifies it even more. Then, on Sunday, you'll be able to make more eye contact with your congregation

7. It helps you know what to cut. You'll be able to identify any boring illustrations or unnecessary information.

Rehearsing also exposes grammatical and sentence structure errors, and shifts in verb and pronoun tense. You may not have noticed these in written form, but they come to you through your hearing.

After "preaching" your sermon, ask your friend the following questions:

- Did my introductory story grab your attention, or did it fizzle?

- Does the story naturally fit and complement the text, or do I need to search for another story that connects better?

- Can you identify my Sermon Summary Sentence in my message?

- Does my Sermon Summary Sentence connect with the "Reveal" of my attention-grabbing story?

- Were you clear on why this message is relevant to your life? Do you think others will be clear on this too?

- Did I include adequate references, statistics, background, and research nuggets? Do you think I need to incorporate additional "proof"?

- Will the diversity of people in our congregation feel they have had their questions answered?

- Do you think the audience will feel affirmed, understood and cared for?

- Could you identify a distinct actionable item, or two, of how this sermon can be put into practice?

- Is my conclusion convincing, or lackluster? Do you think the congregation will feel encouraged to press through their battles with the flesh when they walk out the door into "real life?"

- Overall, do you think this message will touch the hearts of the diverse people in our congregation?

You can also ask your friend, after this process is complete, to affirm or even brainstorm a title for your sermon.

Reverend David M. Ford writes that there is an important psychological reason for practicing your sermon with another

[handwritten: YES!!! I have more "nerves" in front of my family!]

person. People are typically more <u>nervous</u> and <u>self-aware</u> before those to whom they are close, rather than before a larger group of people to whom they are not so close. If you can get through your sermon with a close friend, you'll be able to deliver your message in front of a crowd with confidence.

Your friend will probably be more than happy to offer comments and suggestions afterward as well. Some you may want to consider, and others you might choose to ignore. Be prepared for—and even ask for —constructive criticism. If you find it useful, use it.

Practice What You Preach— Literally!

Your friend has helped you refine your sermon. Now, I suggest you practice it a number of times again before actually preaching it to us on Sunday. You know what you will say, but now you need to spend time considering *how* you will say it.

A producer of one 30-second "spot" commercial takes an astonishing number of "takes" until he reaches a flawless end product. You may need to practice your sermon many times before it is ready for your audiences' ears.

Some pastors tape themselves preaching their sermon before actually presenting it. This is helpful in noticing odd behaviors or nervous habits you may not realize you are doing. Watching a pastor pace back and forth or continually sip water can annoy someone to the point that they do not pay attention to the message. Critique yourself and look for:

- Areas where you need to say something in a softer, more receivable tone.

- Distracting behavior or nervous habits that might detract from the message.

- Any *um's, uh's* or *ah's*.

- Any areas where you talk too fast or too quiet.

- Points in the message where the transition from one point to another is absent or unclear.

Particular sections may need closer attention, such as your very first sentence. If you stumble over your first few words, you may lose the congregation for the rest of the service. Likewise, focus on your conclusion. These are the last words your congregation hears, and you want them to be powerful. Pay attention to how these parts of your message *sound* when you preach them.

Sometimes, you won't know to refine something until you practice it out loud. As you speak your message, ask yourself the following:

- Are there areas I need to pay attention to how I use my body and voice? How can my body and voice reinforce certain words or concepts?

- Are there certain words in my sermon I need to communicate with more enthusiasm, or a convicting tone? What about gestures?

- Are there certain words that need a softer tone?

- Are there places in my message where a few additional seconds of silence could help pack a punch?

Find out what method works best for you. You may want to practice three times back to back on Friday afternoon. Or, you may realize it is better to practice a few times over the course of many days.

Dr. Charles Stone, lead pastor at West Park Church in Ontario, Canada describes his method of practicing for Sunday's message like this: "I go to an upstairs closet in the church on Thursday and preach it out loud once. Then, on Friday, I slowly and silently review it, further tweaking it. On Saturday, I preach it out loud in my bedroom closet. On Sunday morning, I practice it out loud one more time in my closet."

If the only space you have to practice your message privately is a bedroom closet, go for it. If you can practice your message once in the actual venue you be preaching at on Sunday, even better. Whatever you do, practice. As I have said, the pastor's call to preach is a high responsibility. Do it well, and strive for excellence.

"The pulpit, by far, is the largest continuing contact point between pastors and their flocks. It is not the place for a shabby witness." — **Pastor Rolland R. Reece, Rehearsing Your Sermon, 1988**

Chapter Summary:

Once you have finished the outline of your sermon, review it with a trusted friend. Make sure he understands the 7 structural pillars of sermon preparation we have reviewed in this book. Ask him to make sure you have each included (or have been sensitive to) each element in your sermon. Then, practice your sermon as many times as necessary to refine how your message will "sound" when you preach it on Sunday. Help us show confidence in you by the way you project when preaching the Word.

Take our survey at SermonToBook.com to see if your sermons are ready for a book!

The Necessity of Prayer

"A man can preach no better than he prays." — **Charles Stanley**

No matter how much preparation and persuasive material a pastor comes up with, if he isn't communing with God on a continual basis, the message will ring a hollow tune. The pastor needs to hit his knees, let the Spirit lead him, and have a team of dedicated people praying that he'd be soaking up Christ like a sponge and pouring it out on his congregation each week.

Pastors face many challenges caring for the flock God has entrusted to them. The demands are often intense, the job description crosses over into many different areas, people are sometimes dissatisfied (even angry) and the list of needs and hurts is never-ending. One of the most helpful and necessary things for a pastor to do is gather a group of committed people to pray for him, for the ministry, and for the congregation.

In Exodus 17, Joshua and the Israelites were fighting their enemies, the Amalekites, in the Valley of Rephidim. Moses stood on top of a hill, watching, with his staff in his hands. As long as Moses held up his arms, the Israelites continued to win; when his arms grew tired and lowered, the Israelites experienced defeat. Aaron, Moses' brother, and Hur held up Moses' hands until the Israelite army overcame the Amalekites.

You, too, need a few people who will come alongside you and hold you up in prayer, so you can face and win the battles that you and your congregation will face, *together*. Your arms *will* grow tired. You need a prayer team.

Gather a Prayer Team

Paul wrote to his disciple Timothy, "I urge, then, first of all, that petitions, prayers, intercession and thanksgiving be made for all people—for kings and all those in authority, that we may live peaceful and quiet lives in all godliness and holiness. This is good, and pleases God our Savior" (1 Timothy 2:1-3 NIV). He was clear on the necessity to pray for those in authority. Paul also wrote to the Thessalonians that it is God's will that we pray for our spiritual leaders (1 Thessalonians 5:25).

Though it might feel awkward to ask a group of people to pray just for you, it is biblical. And it is imperative for both unity in the body and for the health of your ministry. Dietrich Bonhoeffer writes, "A Christian fellowship lives and exists by the intercession of its members for one another, or it collapses."

Stop for a moment and jot down a list of people who could be part of your prayer team—people who are gifted in the area of prayer in a way others in your congregation may not be. Another trait to watch for is if they can be trusted with sensitive information. The last thing you want is for your prayer warriors to be gossips.

The first step in gathering your team is to ask God for wisdom and discernment. As you are seeking His direction, make a list of the following:

- People who are following the Lord.

- People who believe in the power of prayer.

- People who are humble by nature.

- People you could ask to pray for you on a personal level.

- People who are trusted confidants. You need to know that what you share with your prayer team will not be "leaked" out for the world to know.

- People who are dedicated to consistent prayer. These are the people who are most likely praying for you already, whether you've asked them to or not.

How Do I Organize My Prayer Team?

There are endless ways you can run your prayer team. Typically, teams meet once a week corporately to pray. Come prepared with specific prayer requests and concrete ways that your team can lift you up to God. For example, ask them to pray for your sermon preparation, and for those who may hear it the following Sunday. Ask them to pray that God would move powerfully in lives as a result. Ask them to pray for your purity, your patience, your compassion, your faith, your desire for God, and anything else that might be burdening your heart at the moment.

Appoint one person to lead the team. Instruct this person to send out encouragement and updates to team members via email, and provide tools and resources that might help the team pray for you and your congregation.

It is significant for the supporters to receive prayer updates. These updates can also serve as discipleship tools. As you share stories of transformation in the lives of the people in your congregation, encourage your prayer team members to continue praying for the lost.

"No learning can make up for the failure to pray. No earnestness, no diligence, no study, no gifts will supply its lack." — E.M. Bounds

In developing your prayer team, ask yourself what you hope to accomplish through it. It must be more than a list of requests. Your prayer time should be focused more on God than on yourself and your needs. Yes, you need prayer. But God should be the ultimate focus. Keeping God at the center of your prayer team results in effective and purposeful prayer that makes a difference.

Consider sharing the following with your team, as a grid for the pastoral prayer team ministry:

- Prayer is the only way spiritual leaders can fulfill their accountability to God (James 3:1).

- Prayer is the best defense against Satan's loathing of spiritual leaders (1 Peter 5:8).

- Prayer is indispensable, because of the pastor's susceptibility and influence (1 Samuel 12:13-14).

- Prayer is crucial for the effectiveness of the pastor's ministry (Jeremiah 32:17).

Prayer is a means of acknowledging God's grace, faithfulness, forgiveness and work in both the pastor's and the congregation's life. It helps the pastor keep God's rightful, sovereign place in his own life, and the lives God has called him to shepherd, and it invites God in to everything the pastor does. Though you directly receive blessings from having a team that prays for and with you, ultimately, prayer keeps everyone focused on God.

Pastors need to know that people are praying for him and supporting him to be an effective leader of the church. The enemy's schemes will not be able to stand against the prayers of God's people. Hold firm to what the Word of God promises: "The prayer of a righteous person is powerful and effective" (James 5:16b, NIV).

The apostle Paul lists out some specifics of how the prayer team can pray for you:

"The saying is trustworthy: If anyone aspires to the office of overseer, he desires a noble task. Therefore an overseer

must be above reproach, the husband of one wife, sober-minded, self-controlled, respectable, hospitable, able to teach, not a drunkard, not violent but gentle, not quarrelsome, not a lover of money. He must manage his own household well, with all dignity keeping his children submissive, for if someone does not know how to manage his own household, how will he care for God's church? He must not be a recent convert, or he may become puffed up with conceit and fall into the condemnation of the devil. Moreover, he must be well thought of by outsiders, so that he may not fall into disgrace, into a snare of the devil." — **1 Timothy 3:1-7**

God established you for a kingdom purpose: to shepherd God's flock. Prayer is vital for you to be prepared to lead well and to undergird your sermon preparation each week. It results in blessing for both you and your listeners.

"A prepared messenger is more important than a prepared message." — ***Robert Munger***

Chapter Summary:

I don't have to tell you that pastoring a church has many challenges, which is why God calls others to join in prayer for those He has placed in authority over His flocks. Don't hesitate to gather a prayer team to present to God your needs, the needs of other ministries and ministry leaders, and the needs of the congregation. This team undergirds your sermon each week with prayer.

Ask trustworthy people who are gifted in prayer to join your team. Establish a weekly time to meet, but work out a system to update your prayer team throughout the week as well. A prayer team is essential for you to run the race set out before you (Hebrews 12:1). It blesses you, and it blesses congregation.

Take our survey at <u>SermonToBook.com</u> to see if your sermons are ready for a book!

Conclusion

Together we have looked at the benefits of following the 7 structural pillars of sermon preparation. These pillars not only win back countless wasted hours in your week, but also result in a sermon you can preach with confidence.

Your introduction is compelling and grabs our attention because you have considered our pain, our sin our need for Christ. You have "hooked" us with a powerful story or illustration.

Your *Sermon Summary Sentence* rest snugly in your back pocket, and undergirds everything you preach that day.

Your message reflects why what you are sharing is important for us as individuals. We are sold on the "why" because you have offered us plenty of supporting proof: facts, statistics, and quotations.

We leave with few, if any, questions because you have pre-thought these possible questions out and included answers, settling our hearts.

We go home motivated to do what you have exhorted us to do because you have shown us how to apply your sermon in our everyday lives. And your final words to us resound in our minds not just for the rest of the day, but for the whole week leading up to the next Sunday when you preach again.

When painstaking and deliberate preparation and Spirit dependence collide, the result is an encounter between God's pastor, God's Word and God's people. *This is where excellent preaching is found.*

I am hopeful the simple act of scheduling your sermons for the year transforms not only each week as you prepare, but your entire life. My prayer for you is that the hours saved are redirected into the lives of those you love. My greatest desire is that by embracing these tips and tools you become a better father, husband, son, friend, and pastor.

You, pastor, reflect the heart of Christ to your congregation. You are a witness for Jesus, but sometimes you bear the ugly burden of dealing with people. I pray that when criticism hits, some of the reminders I've offered encourage you to cling to the knowledge of who you are in Christ—not what someone is complaining about. Stand firm and let nothing move you. Even when being criticized, "your labor in the Lord is not in vain" (1 Corinthians 15:58).

Above all, enjoy the process. As you pray, plan, practice and present your sermon, you can be sure there is at least one person who will be impacted by your message: *You.* Amen

Take our survey at SermonToBook.com to see if your sermons are ready for a book!

Appendix A—Conquer Time Management and Boost Productivity

There are two significant reasons why pastors struggle to stay productive: a lack of motivation and miscellaneous distractions. Making just a few changes to your office and the way you organize your day can save countless precious hours, minimize stress, and lead to a much more enjoyable sermon planning process. Your family and congregation reap the benefits too.

Just Sit Down and Do It

No more excuses. Sit down at your desk, and do what needs to be done. Your stress level instantly decreases because you'll be doing the task you are supposed to be doing. If you still find yourself having trouble, think about the reasons why you love your ministry. Even if it's the most boring text in the world, search for a reason to love it and focus on that.

Now, let's move on to building the ideal work environment to make you as productive as possible.

Eliminate Distractions

Emails, texts, phone calls, social media, instant messages, and the Internet, in general, constantly woos you away from working on your sermon if you do not remove them. When it is time to study, close your inbox, vowing only to check it at predetermined times during the day. Sign out of all instant messengers. Turn your phone on silent. And so on.

Any skill you obtain requires practice to fine-tune. The concept of boosting your productivity is no different. Even the most productive people become distracted on a daily basis. They simply know how to shut it down so they don't spiral into an endless social media binge.

Below are some other things to consider, which improves work environments and makes them more productive.

Ergonomic Desk, Keyboard, and Chair. When you are comfortable, you are more productive. If you are not comfortable in your chair, you'll waste time adjusting and readjusting yourself, and those are minutes—if not hours—that are meant for productivity. In the same way, ergonomic keyboards reduce the possibility of repetitive motion injuries, which could severely impact your productivity.

Proper lighting. If you work with dim lighting, you may strain your eyes, which can lead to headaches and fatigue. If you're working in an environment that is too dark, your energy levels may decrease. These factors may seem insignificant, but they can contribute to a lack of productivity.

Quiet environment. When the environment around you is quiet, you can focus wholly on your sermon prep, rather than the loud construction work outside or Vacation Bible School activities. If removing sound is impossible, invest in a headset to block out noise. You can turn on nature sounds, white noise, or music, so long as it doesn't distract you.

Organization. Being organized also helps keep you productive. When everything has a place, you won't waste valuable time looking for something. How you set up your office is up to you. An organizational system that works for one pastor may not work for you. Here are just a few ideas:

- Keep a pen and paper on your desk to jot down notes as miscellaneous things come up throughout the day. (i.e. reminders to call people back, counseling session appointments, prayer requests, etc.)

- Take an initial chunk of time to organize your email inbox each day. You'll save yourself a lot of time in the long run when you are able to find specific emails at the click of a button.

- At the end of your day, write a to-do list for the next day. This helps you focus your attention on the most pertinent tasks the moment you arrive at your office.

- Keep your daily to-do list manageable (five items or less). A massive to-do list will only overwhelm you. Do not borrow tomorrow's worries (or work).

- Complete the tasks you dread the most. With those out of the way, you'll feel more accomplished. Then, as you move through your day, the rest of your tasks are easier to tick off.

- Make specific and detailed deadlines. Be strict with yourself. Tell yourself you will finish a certain project at a certain time, not just "sometime before Sunday morning." This allows more flexibility in your schedule.

  Respond to emails the moment you receive them. Most people have to read an email at least twice—once when it arrives, then again whenever they get around to replying to it. To avoid reading it twice, respond when it's fresh on your mind.

- Most importantly, seek help from others. When Moses was leading the Israelites, who had grown massively in number, his father-in-law, Jethro, stepped in. Jethro spoke truth to Moses, telling him the way he was leading was not effective because he was doing it alone.

"What you are doing is not good. You and the people with you will certainly wear yourselves out, for the thing is too heavy for you. You are not able to do it alone. Now obey my voice; I will give you advice, and God be with you! You shall represent the people before God and bring their cases to God, and you shall warn them about the statutes and the laws, and make them know the way in which they must walk and what they must do. Moreover, look for able men from all the people, men who fear God, who are trustworthy and hate a bribe, and place such men over the people as chiefs of thousands, of hundreds, of fifties, and of tens. And let them judge the people at all times. Every great matter they shall bring to you, but any small matter they shall decide themselves. So it will be easier for you, and they will bear the burden with you." — **Exodus 18:13-22**

Then Jethro told Moses that if he followed these instructions, God would direct him. His job would be easier because others would help carry the burden, and he would be able to endure the task ahead. In the same way, adapting a Lone Ranger attitude will be to your disadvantage. God has likely surrounded you with many people who are ready and willing to help you. Don't miss the blessing of watching God work through others.

10 Tips to Make Your Sermon Prep Time More Productive

In addition to creating a calm, quiet organized and ergonomically efficient work environment, here are some other simple tips that, if followed, will expand your productivity:

1. Don't overload yourself. Remember, you're only one person. As a minister of the gospel, you are already playing several roles. You should not be doing the work of 20.

2. Set clear boundaries. During times of busyness, it's tempting to work straight through weekends and holidays. This intense schedule may be necessary on occasion, but it should never be a regular habit. Weekends and holidays should be reserved for family.

3. Set work hours. While you do have the freedom to make your own schedule, depending on your current ministry load, try to set regular work hours for yourself. Once you settle on your schedule, refrain from running errands during work hours. Certain chores can wait until after you've checked off your to-do list.

4. Refrain from email and social media. Though email and social media are critical parts of ministry, if you're not careful, they can be tremendous time wasters. Set aside a specific time to read and reply to your messages, then close all email and social media tabs and work on your message.

5. Outsource what you don't have time to finish. For example, if you are trying to finish your church website, but don't have a clue about graphic design, seek help from a web designer in your church.

6. Avoid multitasking. Though it may *seem* like you are getting more accomplished, multi-tasking is counterproductive. Research shows that when the brain multitasks, less attention is spread to the individual tasks, making it easier to get distracted and make mistakes. Instead, choose one task at a time until you're finished with your list. Also, try to clump similar tasks together.

7. Use time management tools. There are thousands of time management tools available today. Try some and see which ones work best for you.

8. Ruthlessly prioritize. Learn to cut out what is not important. Make a list of all the things that you need to get done, then think through each one and decide if it is worth your time or not. If not, cut it from the list.

9. Learn to say no. This is your greatest ally. Practice saying no in polite but firm ways. Not always, of course. Your ministry includes a lot of service and spontaneity. But there are times you must decline requests.

10. Rest, eat well, and exercise. Self-care is vital to productivity. Without a healthy mind and body, you will struggle to run on all-cylinders. Don't let an unhealthy lifestyle keep you from ministering to your flock to your full potential.

Appendix B—Browser Add-Ons

When conducting online research, set yourself up for success with browser add-ons. Options vary depending on browser, so I'll cover the two most popular ones: Google Chrome and Mozilla Firefox.

Google Chrome Add-Ons

StayFocusd

This allows you to limit the time you spend on certain websites. Is Facebook killing your productivity? Add it to the list on this add-on, and you'll be kicked off the site once you've hit your time limit. If you really need to buckle down, use the "Nuclear Option" to block time-wasting websites altogether, limiting your browsing capacity only to the websites you need.

Cool Clock

This handy browser add-on gives you a clock, calendar, hourly desktop time notifications, an alarm, and a timer. Find out how long it takes you to do a certain task. Remind yourself when it's time to move on to the next item on your to-do list.

The more productive you are when you don't need to be, the more ready you'll be for drop-ins and emergency-situation ministries.

Todo.ly

This is a task management tool. Use this to make your nightly to-do list, and manage it online from anywhere. Need to work on the go? Forgot your to-do list? Computer crash? No problem! Simply log in to your account and your to-do list is safe.

Mozilla Firefox Add-Ons

Idderall

This is the same thing as StayFocusd for Chrome. It helps you block time-wasting websites, so you can focus on getting your tasks accomplished.

Simple Timer

Simple Timer tracks how long you're spending on various tasks every day. It'll help you see how you're managing your time (i.e. how long you're perusing Facebook, Twitter, blogs, etc.). It could also be useful in calculating the amount of time you are spending on sermon prep and other parts of your ministry.

Prevent Tab Overflow

If you're doing anything online that requires multiple tabs open, it can be time consuming to constantly bounce back and forth trying to find the tab you need. With this add-on, all of your tabs stay visible, so you do not have to waste time scrolling through everything. Keep in mind, however, the more tabs you have open, the slower your computer/browser typically runs. You are usually better off with fewer tabs open.

Appendix C—Taking Care of Your Emotional and Spiritual Health

Pastors often push aside their own spiritual, mental and emotional health. Unfortunately, unhealthy pastors do not serve their congregations and communities well.

Data is limited, but research indicates some of the most critical issues facing clergy today appear to be in the areas of obesity, mental health, heart disease and stress. *The Barna Group* reports that:

- Ninety percent of clergy work between 55 and 75 hours per week.

- Fifty percent of pastors report feeling unable to meet the demands of their jobs.

- Seventy percent of pastors surveyed said they continually fight depression.

- Fifty percent of new pastors do not last five years.

- Twenty-five percent of pastors said they have nowhere to go to if they have a personal or family conflict or concern.

- Thirty-three percent of pastors said they have no established means of resolving conflict.

- Sixty percent of pastors believe that church ministry has negatively impacted their passion for church work.

- Fifty percent of pastors' marriages end in divorce.

- Seventy percent of pastors do not have a close friend.

- Forty percent of pastors said they have no place for outside renewal like a family vacation or continuing education.

- At any given time, 2,000 pastors in America want to quit.

These are sobering statistics. The people God has established to lead His flocks are barely hanging on. If drastic lifestyle and ministry changes are not made, the retention rate of pastors will continue to decline.

The potential work ahead of you always exceeds what you can accomplish. Take control of your health by acknowledging this, and stop trying to "do it all."

As a pastor, you have to fight for your spiritual, physical and emotional health. Do not give the devil a foothold!

Below are some simple yet potentially life-altering tips to consider implementing in your life:

Set realistic expectations. People will always be quick to let you know when you have failed. Set your expectations, and don't allow another person's unmet expectation affect you.

Enlist someone to be your gatekeeper. This person can be an administrative assistant, fellow pastor or spouse. This person should filter the masses of negative criticism that may come your way, through email or phone, to prevent you from becoming bogged down with negativity.

Take time away from the church or your place of ministry to refuel and decompress. Workaholism leads to burnout, which can quickly lead to depression. Put aside any guilt for taking time off, and remind yourself that taking a break is essential for your overall mental and physical health.

Prioritize immediate family over church family. Tend to any marriage or family problems immediately. Your congregation should never take precedence over your role as husband, father, or son.

Manage finances well. Financial stress can lead to anxiety and/or depression. Do not let pride get in the way of learning to handle money better. Seek help if needed.

Guard against comparison. Comparing your congregation to others can be debilitating for some pastors. Focus on the flock God has called you to and trust Him for everything else.

Maintain an active relationship with an accountability partner. Give this person permission to speak truth to you, especially if they see you making poor choices that affect your health.

Care for your body. Eat nutritiously, exercise regularly, get adequate rest and sleep and schedule regular physical exams.

Expectations and demands upon a pastor are colossal, which is why burnout, depression and other serious health problems are so prevalent. The enemy does not want pastors to thrive in their ministries, so he does whatever he can to prey on their weak areas, to prevent the gospel from being preached.

Pastors today must voraciously guard their physical, emotional and spiritual health. There is too much at stake not to!

"He gives strength to the weary and increases the power of the weak. Even youths grow tired and weary, and young men stumble and fall; but those who hope in the LORD will renew their strength. They will soar on wings like eagles; they will run and not grow weary, they will walk and not be faint." — **Isaiah 40:29-31**

Appendix D—Online Resources for Pastors

"Always be learning! Let the Bible speak for itself and be your platform. Listen to other preachers as much as you can. I'll say what other preachers have said all the time. Podcasts are the common day commentaries. Surround yourself with people who can help you communicate better. Get a great team to support you as the preacher. Don't 'give them hell' on Sunday. 'Give them hope' on Sunday.'"
— **Perry Noble**

The following are just a few helpful online resources to help you in sermon preparation.

Preaching Rocket. Preaching Rocket is a revolutionary, step-by-step system designed to take the stress and worry out of creating powerful sermons each week. This site offers helpful videos, articles, and audio downloads for pastors. http://resources.therocketcompany.com/

SermonAudio. Sermon Audio is the largest and most trusted library of over 980,000 free audio sermons from conservative Christian churches and ministries worldwide. They offer audio and webcast sermons by book of the Bible, topic and speaker. http://www.sermonaudio.com/main.asp

Sermon Illustrations. Sermon Illustrations is a helpful website that lists sermon illustrations alphabetically by topic. http://www.sermonillustrations.com/

WorkingPreacher: This site produced by Luther Seminary offers brief commentary and extensive podcasts. http://www.workingpreacher.org/default.aspx

Nasa Gallery. This website by NASA provides a magnificent gallery of royalty-free photos taken by NASA, including satellite imagery, historical moments, aeronautical aircraft, weather phenomena, planets, nebulae, and other amazing images of the cosmos. It is perfect for topics like creation, perspective, humility, and God's power and majesty. http://www.nasa.gov/multimedia/imagegallery/index.html

TextWeek. TextWeek is the largest and best catalog of links to Scripture resources, online commentaries, sample sermons, liturgical ideas, sample prayers and litanies, children's resources, and just about everything you can think of. It is well designed and well maintained. http://www.textweek.com/

GrowChurches. GrowChurches is an online community and resource for pastors and leaders. Topics include church growth, Christian leadership training and evangelism. http://growchurch.net/

Pastors.com. Pastors.com hosts resources, leadership advice, and content for leaders as well as a forum for the global church. http://pastors.com/

CrossWalk. CrossWalk provides resources for pastors and the general Christian community such as devotionals, articles, blogs and videos. www.crosswalk.com

IMdB: The Internet Movie Database. This site has comprehensive information for every film you can think of, whether high- or low profile, big-league or independent producers, Christian or otherwise. My favorite information for sermon prep is their behind-the-scenes trivia on films, as well as their movie quotation database, which is searchable by keyword. http://www.imdb.com/

MinistryMatters. This website provides a wealth of information on preaching, teaching, and worship. The Preaching and Worship sections have a sidebar where resources for each upcoming Sunday are grouped together. http://www.ministrymatters.com/

Gallup Polls. Most are familiar with Gallup's data-driven news and poll results on human behavior and popular culture. Its extensive database of results is constantly updated, and you can have regular updates on your topic of choice sent directly to your email address. Try the topics "Moral Issues" or "Religion" for church-relevant data. (George Gallup and George Gallup Jr., like George Barna, are committed followers of Christ.) http://www.gallup.com/home.aspx

Guinness Book of World Records. It's hard to forget an illustration supported by a woman with 24-foot-long fingernails or a guy who stood on one foot for 3 solid days. This is my favorite site to use when researching commitment, loyalty, dedication, uniqueness or success.

<u>http://www.guinnessworldrecords.com/</u>

Appendix E—Checklist of Action Items

Get a prayer team started: Start by asking God for direction, as you carefully select trustworthy people in your church to join your prayer team. Identify one person to lead the team, and instruct him/her to be in charge of setting meeting dates, communicating with the team, and sending out information to equip and encourage the team.

Decide on a text: Start by asking God what scriptural truth He wants you to communicate to your congregation each time you preach. Once you've identified the text, spend time doing word studies and examining cross-references. Guard against taking Scripture out of context—what you preach on must be filtered through the whole council of God. Make sure to preach consistently from both the Old and New Testaments. Keep a running list of topics you would like to preach on in the future, and add to this list as God leads.

Write an attention-grabbing story: Write a strong, attention-grabbing story by crafting three paragraphs: the *Setup*, the *Incident*, and the *Reveal*. First, write a setup paragraph. Orient your congregation to the 5 W's of your story: *Who, What, Where, When, and Why*. Second, describe the incident. Here you express what happens in the story that sets up the point you want to make. Finally, craft the "reveal." This is where you write about how the story connects to the overall point of your message.

Incorporate more reading into your day: Choose one or two magazines and keep them in your car. Make a point to read them when you are waiting in the car, checkout line, or doctor's office. Do the same thing with books. Schedule a few hours on your work calendar each week specifically to read. If it's not scheduled, it probably won't happen. Transfer time you may spend in front of the television into reading time. Download books from Audible.com or www.christianbook.com/page/audiobooks and listen to them while you are at the gym or on your lunch hour. Order books on CDs and listen to them when driving, especially if you have a long commute. Consider other windows of time in which you are doing nothing in particular but could be reading. Soon, reading will become a habit.

Create a system for finding and filing stories: Google Evernote's "Getting Started" page. Spend time learning the system, and consider using it as a means of taking notes, storing articles, story ideas, and photos that you can use in a future sermon. With Evernote, you can create "Notebooks" by topic and store stories accordingly. You can even create a file labeled "Sermon Story Ideas," and add ideas to it as you come across them. Create tabs for specific topics such as Marriage, Parenting, Eschatology, Easter, Giving, or Sin. This way, your stories are organized by topic and easily accessible when you need them.

Conduct an online search for sermon illustrations: Schedule a few hours a week to search for sermon illustrations online. Search by topic and add them to your filing system. Don't limit yourself to stories; use this time to search for related quotes, analogies, and even corresponding images that can be used on Power Point to bring a visual image to the story you plan to tell. Search for anecdotes, stories, blog entries, editorial opinions, famous tweets, historical events, memorable sayings, biographical profiles, statistics, or TV interview snippets. File them in your new filing system.

Gather personal stories for sermon illustrations: Reflect on personal stories that could serve as helpful sermon illustrations. Ask your spouse to help you remember funny, interesting, or difficult events in your life (or your family's life) that correlates with your message topic. Ask your friends, parents, or grandparents to reflect on your experiences as a child or a young adult and see if they could be used as a lesson or an analogy. Even if you can't use these stories at the moment, file them away. You never know when they might become the perfect attention-grabber for your message.

Create a sermon summary sentence: Create a sentence that is simple enough for a child to understand, yet embodies the crux of your message. (If it helps, think of the first three words that come to mind when you think about the passage). Then construct a simple sentence that is catchy, proverbial and memorable—one that "sticks." Does it describe your entire message? If so, you have succeeded!

Make sure your listeners understand why: Write down the top three ways your message benefits your audience. Write a 'blessings' paragraph based on these three reasons, then write a 'consequences' paragraph based on the opposites of those three reasons. Doing this exercise should clarify why it is important for your listeners to understand your message and why it is beneficial for their lives.

Identify the backbone of your message: Write down at least three core verses, three quotes, and one statistic/research nugget that serve as the backbone of your message. Then write a paragraph that sums up your burden of proof. The strongest "proof" you have in your message is the Scripture you use—the ultimate backbone of your entire message. Online lexicons and concordances make this step easy. Make sure when you include supporting Scripture that you keep verses in context, and always explain any confusing portions. Study and meditate on every verse you include, and ask God to reveal whether or not they truly support your message.

Organize your commentaries: Post a list of online commentaries near your computer (for easy access), or bookmark the links for online commentaries so you never waste time searching for them. If you prefer hard copies, keep a set of commentaries near your computer. There are complete Bible commentaries available in one large volume. If you don't own a commentary like this, phone your local used bookstores to see if they have any for sale, order used sets off Amazon, or look on Craig's List. Tab certain topics you plan to refer to often (for quick reference). Do the same with the devotionals you return to frequently.

Articulate your listener's questions: Think of any questions your audience might already be asking before they ask. Step into their shoes and ask yourself what emotions they might be feeling, (i.e. what parts of your message might be stirring up disagreement or confusion in them).

Example: When preaching on homosexuality, someone in the audience may be thinking: *What about my son, who just told me he is bisexual? How do I navigate around the sin, but still love him?*

Deal with doctrinal differences: Voice any doctrinal differences you think may arise, especially if it is a sensitive subject. Feel free to state your own theological position, but always encourage your congregation to study the Scriptures on their own. This should be done with gray areas of Scripture only, not the non-negotiable pillars of the Christian faith.

Example: If you hold a Calvinist view of salvation regarding the elect, you may also want to suggest that many others hold an Arminian view. State your reasons why you believe what you do, but encourage your congregation to study the Scriptures themselves and come up with their own theology on this topic.

Simplify word choice: Check to make sure there are no large "Christianese" words in your message. Scan your draft and see if any words end with "ation", such as *sanctification, justification* or *regeneration.* Either replace them with words a middle-school student would understand, or make sure to explain the terms adequately.

Acknowledge deep hurt: Ask yourself what emotions your message might evoke. Will your topic stir up deep-seeded hurt in your listeners? If so, fervently ask the Holy Spirit to council you on how to handle the harsher truths with compassion, discernment, and above all, empathy. Include a sentence or two that lets people know they're not alone in their guilt or hurt.

Example: Suppose your message touches on the subject of abortion. Instead of dropping an emotional bomb by simply saying God values all life and hates abortion, acknowledge that there are many in the room that either know someone who has had an abortion, or perhaps have had one themselves. Include a reminder of God's grace, and His ability to make all things new. Encourage them that they are not alone. Make yourself available to meet with those hurting outside of the Sunday service, or suggest some resources.

Preach to different learning styles: Review your sermon for the coming week, and make sure you have included at least four different modes of learning throughout your message. It's okay to preach "lecture style," but intersperse your message with other tools to reach the following types of learners: *visual/spatial, musical/auditory, physical/kinesthetic, solitary, logical/mathematical, and verbal.*

Example: Engage both the musical/auditory learners and the physical/kinesthetic learners by asking a member from the congregation gifted in dancing to perform to a worship song with lyrics related to the topic you are preaching on. Even better, reach visual learners by having the lyrics scroll across the screen on Power Point in sync with the dance performance.

Create action items: Conclude your sermon with clear action items to help your audience know how to apply the main point of your message. Write out your Sermon Summary Sentence. Is your sermon subject timeless? Does it address different types and ages of people? If the answer is yes, next formulate clear action items through the lens of your diverse congregation. In order of importance, write down some specific actions you want your congregation to take with them into their week.

Example: Let's say your message focuses on Romans 10:9: "If you declare with your mouth, 'Jesus is Lord,' and believe in your heart that God raised him from the dead, you will be saved." A strong action item for the unbeliever could be, "If you have never declared Jesus to be Lord, and you believe that He indeed is your Savior, don't wait! Tell somebody what you believe." However, for the long-time believer this may not be a moving action point. So to encourage both types of people, you might also say, "And maybe you have been walking with Jesus for many years. You too can declare your belief in Jesus to someone! This not only solidifies your own belief, but may encourage someone else who is on the fence."

Do a heart check on yourself: You are asking your listeners to move on some action items. Make sure you are living out what you are asking your audience to live out! There is nothing more discouraging (and confusing) than a pastor who walks the road of hypocrisy, preaching one thing but living life in a completely different (or sinful) way.

Example: Your message discusses the body being a temple of the Holy Spirit. You've included some concrete examples of ways to keep this temple "pure," and you've mentioned the use of foul language, and quoted Luke who wrote, "A good man brings good things out of the good stored up in his heart, and an evil man brings evil things out of the evil stored up in his heart. For the mouth speaks what the heart is full of." However, on the way home someone cuts you off on the road and a rainbow of choice words roll off your tongue.

Avoid weak conclusions: Make sure you wrap up your sermon in the most powerful way possible. Write a conclusion that relates directly to your Sermon Summary Sentence, is unique and memorable, and "lands the plane" smoothly and completely. Restate your main points and then simply stop. Conclusions aren't necessarily the best part of your message, but they are the gate out of which your listeners leave. Spend a few extra minutes planning them out well.

Example: Instead of ending your sermon like this: *"Don't sit back and wait for others to serve you. Serve them! There are many ways to serve others. What are you waiting for?"* Instead, use some strong, open-ended questions, like this: *"How will you reach out to someone who has less than you this week? Who have you served in the past six months out of humility and gratefulness to Jesus?"*

Circle back when writing conclusions: Intentionally leave a story or a quote unfinished, and tell your congregation that you will get back to it later. This will pique their interest. Then fill in the missing portion of the story or quote in a way that brings a final "aha!" to your message. Or reread a quote or story at the end of your message for an added punch.

Take control of your week: Schedule your priorities. Open up your calendar and look at the upcoming month. Write in non-negotiable commitments, starting with family activities first. Schedule date night with your wife, and your kid's sports or school events. Next, schedule your sermon preparation time and let your staff know. Solicit someone—an administrative assistant or even your spouse—to help you protect this preparation time from interruptions. Also, schedule meetings with those in the church who need your pastoral care in the upcoming weeks, and block off time for church administrative needs.

Schedule a weekend away for planning: Block off an entire weekend to get away and plan for the upcoming year. Bring your Bible, computer, related books, your file or binder of sermon illustration ideas, and any ideas your staff has given you for future sermons or sermon series. You may even want to bring a whiteboard and a stand to map out where you plan to take your congregation spiritually through your messages. If you don't have the financial ability to book a hotel, ask a friend or member of the congregation who has vacation property if you could stay at their place. Most people are more than willing to offer material things they are blessed with to help their pastor, especially if they know what you are be doing.

What to consider when creating a sermon calendar: When creating your yearly sermon spreadsheet, make sure to block off the following: preaching dates, holidays, non-religious dates, Scripture texts and their genre, themes, and the time of year and season. Align this calendar with your personal calendar, and make sure to plan for your vacations and guest preachers.

Who to invite into the planning process: Ask God to make it clear to you whom to invite into the planning process once your *Sermon Calendar* is established. Consider asking the following people: board members, the church receptionist, worship team leaders, the graphic designer, the outreach coordinator, and various ministry leaders. Explain to them your system of planning for your sermons, and encourage them to develop a similar system for their particular ministry. Release them to be creative, and remind them that the purpose for doing this is to focus everyone on the same thing, and excite members of the congregation for what's ahead.

Select a preaching team: Identify who this team is, and personally invite them to participate in the planning process. Start by seeking the guidance of the Holy Spirit; ask God to help you select godly, humble and committed leaders to come alongside you in your sermon planning process. Meet with them one-on-one, and explain what you are asking them to commit to. Tell them you are seeing their opinions prior to creating your annual calendar, asking them for suggestions for future sermons, and reading and summarizing a book periodically that you might not be able to read yourself. Tell them you need their honest but godly input, and that this is a vital role in helping to communicate God's truths with excellence.

Reduce the possibility of burnout: Your first priority should be to cultivate a dependence upon God, and next to prioritize your family. If these things fall apart, you simply cannot be an effective (or healthy) pastor. Second, lower your expectations of yourself. Schedule time for rest and relaxation, and connect with other pastors to refuel and reenergize your mission.

When to seek help from a professional: If you find yourself getting angry quickly, irritated over minor issues, overly defensive, or if you think about quitting often or are uptight around your spouse, kids or friends for no apparent reason, you may be need to consider seeking outside help. Put your pride aside, and ask other pastors whom you respect if they have a recommendation for a counselor who can help you work through this season of life.

Be prepared for criticism: Before you receive criticism (and it is inevitable), write down three possible responses to criticism of your messages or leadership. Practice them while you are driving, or in front of a mirror. Imagine yourself responding calmly and with love.

Review your message with a friend: Ask a trusted friend to critique your message—someone who is not afraid of being honest. Present your sermon draft and ask him to suggest areas to either cut or expand, identify unclear sections, bumpy transitions, and so forth. Have your friend rate your introduction, comment on your attention grabbers, and find your Sermon Summary Sentence. Ask him if you included adequate references, statistics, background, and research nuggets, and if he heard clear actionable items. Finally, have him comment on your conclusion. Was it convincing, or lackluster?

Practice your sermon (more than once!): Establish a quiet place where you can practice your sermon more than once. Or plan on practicing a few times over a period of two or three days. Practice it exactly as you plan to deliver it—complete with voice inflections and hand gestures. Make sure to time your message, and pay attention to any nervous habits that you might need to eliminate. Finally, remove any *um's* and *ah's*.

Eliminate potential distractions: Is your office cluttered? Do you feel anxious just looking at the piles of paper on your desk? Remove anything that will become a distraction or add unnecessary stress. Adjust poor lighting, clear your email inbox and invest in an ergonomically correct chair and keyboard to improve comfort. If noise disturbs your concentration, listen to music, ambience, or use earplugs.

Examine your work week: In the last month, how many hours did you spend doing ministry? This includes evening commitments, weekend services, Bible study, counseling sessions, lunches appointments, sermon prep, drop-ins, prayer meetings, church picnics, etc. If the number of hours exceeds what you know is healthy, find ways to cut back. You may even need to make a drastic lifestyle change.

Schedule time to decompress and rejuvenate: Put guilt aside and schedule time in the next month to step away from your commitments at work to relax, decompress and rejuvenate. If you can, plan one night away with your spouse. Let people know ahead of time that you aren't responding to emails or calls until you return. Or plan something fun for the whole family, such as a hike, dinner at your favorite restaurant, or a trip to the beach. It doesn't matter what you do, as long as you are able to fully disengage from your duties as a pastor.

Take steps to improve your health: If your eating and exercise habits have deteriorated, consider a complete lifestyle change. Ask your spouse to help you come up with a strategy to improve your health. For example, commit to a weight management App, such as *Lose It* or *Pact*; take a jog each morning before work; or make healthy lunches instead of buying a Dairy Queen burger on your lunch break. As you begin to implement a healthier regimen, take note of any differences in your energy level and weight. I know it's extremely difficult to maintain a healthy lifestyle, but it will greatly impact you and your ministry.

Thank You

"There should be no question as to the great importance of a proper arrangement of the sermon material." — **William Evans, How to Prepare Sermons**

THANK YOU, DEAR PASTOR, FOR INVESTING in *Sermon Crunch*. My team at SermonToBook.com prays that the 7 pillars serve you well in your ministry.

I am always looking to improve the resources we offer to pastors and I would love to hear your comments about *Sermon Crunch*.

Please write me at info@sermontobook.com or stop by our website. I look forward to serving you in the future!

Take our survey at SermonToBook.com to see if your sermons are ready for a book!

Turning Your Sermons Into Books

Ever thought about turning your sermons into a book? Check us out at SermonToBook.com.

SermonToBook.com began with a simple belief: that sermons should be touching lives, *not* collecting dust. That's why we turn sermons into high-quality books that are accessible to people all over the globe.

Turning your sermon or sermon series into a book exposes more people to God's Word, better equips you for counseling, accelerates future sermon prep, adds credibility to your ministry, and even helps make ends meet during tight times.

John 21:25 tells us that the world itself couldn't contain the books that would be written about the work of Jesus Christ. Our mission is to try anyway. Because, in Heaven, there will no longer be a need for sermons or books. Our time is now.

If God so leads you, we'd love to work with you on your sermon or sermon series.

Visit SermonToBook.com to learn more.

Take our survey at <u>SermonToBook.com</u> to see if your sermons are ready for a book!

- **Impact** your church, community, and the entire world with sermons you've already preached.

- **Discover** how to publish your sermons in less than 1 hour of your time.

- **Learn** the process we use to help pastors fund their books before they are even written.

Book 3: Go to <u>Amazon.com</u> to buy paperback copies of the entire Pastoral Leadership and Church Administration Made Easy Bundle!

Book 2: Go to Amazon.com to buy paperback copies of the entire Pastoral Leadership and Church Administration Made Easy Bundle!

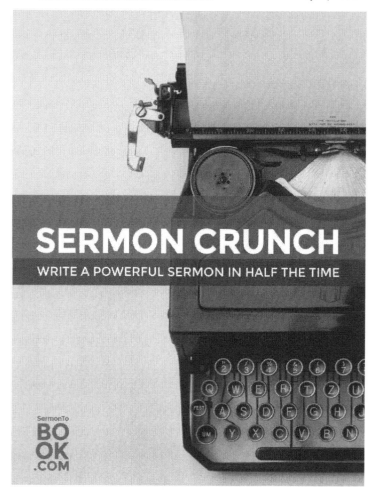

Book 1: Go to Amazon.com to buy paperback copies of the entire Pastoral Leadership and Church Administration Made Easy Bundle!

Made in the USA
Coppell, TX
30 November 2021

66755654R00101